# A Parent's Guide to the Common Core

# Grade 5

© 2014 Kaplan, Inc.

Published by Kaplan Publishing, a division of Kaplan, Inc.
395 Hudson Street
New York, NY 10014

Printed in the United States of America

10 9 8 7 6 5 4 3 2 1

ISBN-13: 978-1-61865-820-3

Kaplan Publishing books are available at special quantity discounts to use for sales promotions, employee premiums, or educational purposes. For more information or to purchase books, please call the Simon & Schuster special sales department at 866-506-1949.

# TABLE OF CONTENTS

# INTRODUCTION TO THE COMMON CORE STANDARDS

This book is designed to introduce you and your child to the Common Core Standards, a major development in the way U.S. students are taught the most basic and critical areas of knowledge that they will encounter while in school. The Common Core Standards will be used to create assessments beginning in the 2014-2015 school year.

## Where did the Common Core Standards come from?

The Common Core Standards were developed to create more uniform academic standards across the United States. Since each state has traditionally created its own academic standards and assessments, students in one state would often end up studying different things than students in another state. Education professionals from across the nation worked together to select the best and most relevant standards from all the states, and then used these as the basis for new standards that could be used by every state to ensure that all students are fully prepared for the future. The Common Core Standards are, in many cases, more comprehensive and demanding than previous state standards. These new standards are designed to help American students perform favorably against students from other developed nations—an area in which the United States has fallen behind in recent years.

The Common Core Standards were not created by the federal government. Each state may choose whether it wishes to use the Common Core Standards, or stick with its own unique learning standards. However, most states have recognized the importance of consistent and high-level standards for all American students. At printing, forty-five states, along with the District of Columbia and four U.S. territories, have adopted the Common Core Standards.

## What are the Common Core Standards?

The Common Core Standards are the standards to which all students will be held. These standards are applicable for grades K-12. The Common Core Standards focus on two areas of learning: English Language Arts and Mathematics. These areas were chosen because they are critical to developing a foundation a solid foundation for learning, and encompass other fields such as social studies and science.

Within English Language Arts, the Common Core Standards are divided into several categories: Reading; Writing; Speaking & Listening; and Language. For Grade 5, reading standards are focused on finding main ideas, analyzing arguments, and comparing and contrasting story elements in reading passages. Writing standards focus on developing arguments that are supported with evidence and information and organized in a logical way. These skills are critical for building a foundation for success, both in school and in later life.

Within Mathematics, the Common Core Standards are also divided into several categories. For Grade 5, these categories are: Operations & Algebraic Thinking; Number & Operations in Base Ten; Number & Operations—Fractions; Measurement & Data; and Geometry. For Grade 5, Number & Operations in Base Ten focuses mainly on understanding place values and decimals, as well as division using area models to illustrate. Number & Operations—Fractions focuses on handling fractions with unlike denominators, as well as multiplication and division of fractions. Measurement & Data focuses on the principles and basics of measuring volumes. These skills have been identified as critical for success in other areas such as the sciences.

The Common Core Standards do not dictate a teacher's curriculum; they just ensure that all teachers are working toward the same learning standards. Teachers were instrumental in developing the standards, and remain the dominant force in helping your child achieve academic potential. However, as a parent, you now have the opportunity to see the "road map" that your child's teachers will be using to build their courses of study. This allows you to better become an active participant in helping your child achieve these learning goals.

## How to use this book

This book is designed to provide you with the tools necessary to help your child succeed. While the Common Core Standards are numerous for each grade level, Kaplan's learning experts have identified the standards that are most critical for success, both in the classroom and on assessment tests. These are known as the "power standards." Each lesson in this book is dedicated to a different power standard. The power standards are also the focus of the tests and quizzes throughout the book.

You should begin by having your child take the Pre-Test for each domain. The Pre-Test is designed to cover the same skills that will likely be tested on state assessments. This will give you an idea of the areas in which your child excels, as well as the areas that may need special attention.

Once you have gauged your child's baseline skills, the lessons offer practical experience with each of the power standards. Each lesson provides information on what the standard means, and offers examples of how the standard might be addressed through classroom teaching and through testing. In addition, each lesson offers an activity that you can engage in with your child to help practice the skills highlighted in the lesson. Once you are confident in your child's abilities with regard to a lesson, you can have your child take the end-of-lesson quiz for that power standard to ensure mastery.

When you have completed all the lessons, have your child complete the Post-Test for each domain. You can compare your child's performance on the Post-Test to the Pre-Test, and see which areas have improved the most. If some areas still need work, re-read the corresponding lesson with your child, and try to pinpoint the specific issue that your child needs additional help mastering. The List of Resources provided with this book includes a number of Web sites, publications, and other types of resources that can help you and your child continue to practice and reinforce the Common Core Standards.

**Common Core State Standards Initiative:** http://www.corestandards.org/.
This Web site offers in-depth information about the Common Core Standards and their history.

**National Library of Virtual Manipulatives:** http://nlvm.usu.edu/en/nav/vlibrary.html.
This National Science Foundation supported project allows students, teachers, and parents to interact with virtual manipulatives that can aid in teaching basic mathematic principles.

**Math Videos by Math Playground:** http://www.mathplayground.com/mathvideos.html.
These videos address a wide range of math-related questions, from "How do you add fractions?" to "How do you solve an inequality?"

**Illustrative Mathematics:** http://www.illustrativemathematics.org/
This educator-designed tool is meant to provide teachers with support and resources for teaching math.

**Inside Mathematics:** http://www.insidemathematics.org/
Like Illustrative Mathematics, this is a resource for professional; however, it offers a wealth of examples for how to present math concepts to students.

**New Common Core Math Problems and Resources:** https://www.khanacademy.org/commoncore.
Khan Academy, one of the world's premier not-for-profit online classrooms, offers practice problems that are mapped to the specific Common Core Standards and organized by grade level.

**Free Activities and Worksheets from Flashkids:** http://www.flashkids.com/free-downloads.
These activities and worksheets are broken down by domain and grade level, and can be a fun way to improve skills critical to Common Core.

**Parents' Guide to Student Success, 5th Grade:** http://pta.org/files/5th%20Grade_B-W.pdf.
This overview from the National Parent-Teacher Association tells you in detail what you should expect from a curriculum aimed at meeting Common Core Standards.

**Parent Roadmaps to the Common Core Standards—English Language Arts:** http://www.cgcs.org/Domain/36.
The Council of the Great City Schools offers parent roadmaps to help you support your child in math and English language arts at each grade level.

**Working with the "Shifts":** http://www.engageny.org/sites/default/files/resource/attachments/parent_workshop_what_parents_can_do_handout.pdf.

This handout from the New York State Education Department explains in detail how the Common Core Standards have shifted the content and methods used by teachers, and offers suggestions for how you can help your student thrive amid these changes.

**Achieve the Core:** http://www.achievethecore.org/.
This Web site was created by the main creators of the Common Core Standards as a way to provide free teaching materials tailored to help students master the skills needed to meet these standards.

**ReadWriteThink Tips & How-To Resources for Parents:** http://www.readwritethink.org/search/?grade 58-12&resource_type574.
This site, supported by the International Reading Association and the National Council of Teachers of English, provides tips to help parents nurture their child's interest in reading and the language arts.

**PBS Parents:** Reading & Language: http://www.pbs.org/parents/education/reading-language/.
This Web site, affiliated with the Public Broadcasting Service (PBS), offers advice for improving your child's literacy and love of reading.

***The Secret Garden*** by Frances Hodgson Burnett.
This classic novel, available in the public domain, is an excellent text for fifth-grade readers. It is considered a prime example of the type of text used to test Common Core Standards.

***Alice's Adventures in Wonderland*** by Lewis Carroll.
Another classic novel available in the public domain, this is considered a prime example of the type of text used to test Common Core Standards.

**American Library Association Summer Reading List, Grades 3-5:** http://www.ala.org/alsc/sites/ala .org.alsc/files/content/SummerReadingList_3-5_BW.pdf.
This list, aimed at keeping kids involved in reading during their summer months, includes titles that are highly recommended by student readers at the same grade level as your child.

# English Language Arts Pre-Test

The pre-test is intended as a preliminary assessment of your child's language arts skills. The questions cover reading comprehension, vocabulary, and writing. There are a variety of question types at various levels of cognition. These are typical of the types of questions that your fifth grader might experience in the classroom, as homework, and in assessment situations.

A grid at the end provides the main Common Core standard assessed, as well as a brief explanation of the correct answers. This is intended to provide information about which standards your child might need the most help with. Because of this, you may want to encourage your child to take an educated guess on questions that he or she is unsure of, but to mark these with a question mark. This will help you identify areas that might need reinforcement.

The items on the pre-test are **not** designed to replicate standardized tests used to assess a child's reading level or a school's progress in helping the child achieve grade level.

## Read the following two paragraphs aloud to your child:

This test includes questions to test reading, vocabulary, and writing skills. Please answer as best as possible. The test will not be graded. If you come across a question that you are unsure of, put a question mark next to it and make your best guess.

Some of the questions are based on stories or other reading passages. Read the passage carefully. If you don't know the answer to a question, look back at the passage to see if you can find it.

*For each section, read the passage and then answer the questions that follow.*

 ## The Aral Sea

The Aral Sea is located between Kazakhstan and Uzbekistan in Central Asia. The lake serves as a catch basin for an enormous region stretching south all the way to Afghanistan. There is very little rainfall around the Aral Sea. Much of its water comes from glacier and snow melt in faraway mountains. Most of this comes by way of two rivers, the Syr Darya and the Amu Darya.

Until recently, the Aral Sea was one of the largest lakes in the world. During the middle of the twentieth century, the area surrounding the Aral Sea was controlled by the Soviet Union.

Soviet leaders felt that the dry grasslands in the region could be better used for farmland that produced crops such as cotton. However, cotton required much more water to grow than natural rainfall could provide. To fix this problem, Soviet engineers created irrigation channels that took water from the rivers that fed the Aral Sea and diverted it to the new cotton fields. However, the irrigation channels that they created were not lined with watertight material. This meant that a substantial portion of the water that passed along these canals was lost into the surrounding soil instead of reaching the crops.

This massive irrigation project robbed the Aral Sea of its main sources of water. Because of this, the Aral Sea began to shrink. The lake also became saltier, which left the remaining water less suitable for drinking and agriculture, and killed off much of its plant and animal life. The increased salt levels permeated the soil in the areas around the lake, making the land unfit for growing crops. In addition, a rapidly increasing population in the region put an even greater strain on the lake as the area's main water supply.

By 2007, the Aral Sea had shrunk by 90 percent. It was no longer a single lake, but four much smaller lakes that looked like the remnants of an evaporating puddle. The exposed lake bed had turned into a salty desert. The waters of the lake once helped to regulate temperatures by absorbing and retaining heat. But now, with nearly all the water gone, the region surrounding the Aral Sea had become hotter in the summer and colder in the winter.

The countries affected by the shrinkage of the Aral Sea have implemented programs in an attempt to reclaim the lake. The most successful is the Dike Kokaral, a levee built to increase water levels in the remaining northern part of the lake. Over the past several years, the water in the North Aral Sea has increased, and the salt levels in the water have decreased. This has allowed some plant and animal life to return, and fishing has once again become a viable industry. Although the South Aral Sea remains in grave danger of disappearing completely, the increase in awareness about the problem may yet pull the lake back from the brink of total environmental disaster.

# Questions

1. In one sentence, summarize the passage.

   _____

   _____

   _____

   _____

2. According to the passage, where is the Aral Sea located?
   A. Syr Darya
   B. Amu Darya
   C. Central Asia
   D. Afghanistan

3. Based on its usage in the second paragraph, which of the following is closest in meaning to the word *diverted*?
   A. changed the course of
   B. blocked off
   C. dug deeper
   D. made plans for

4. What is the main idea of the second paragraph?

_____

_____

_____

_____

5. Based on the passage, what caused plant and animal life to die off?
   A. *Farmers dumped waste into the lake.*
   B. *More people came to live in the area.*
   C. *The weather became hotter.*
   D. *The lake became saltier.*

6. Based on its usage in the third paragraph, which of the following is closest in meaning to the word *permeated*?
   A. *became permanent*
   B. *disappeared from*
   C. *passed into*
   D. *improved*

7. What evidence in the passage supports the idea that the Aral Sea has had an impact on weather in the region?
   A. *The weather became cooler in the summer and warmer in the winter.*
   B. *The weather became warmer in the summer and cooler in the winter.*
   C. *The glaciers stopped melting, and no longer supply water to the lake.*
   D. *The soil became saltier, making it difficult to grow crops.*

8. Based on its usage in the fourth paragraph, which of the following is closest in meaning to the word *remnants*?
   A. *memories*
   B. *pieces of leather*
   C. *shapes*
   D. *remaining parts*

9. Which sentence from the passage best expresses the author's position on the Aral Sea?
   A. *"Although the South Aral Sea remains in grave danger of disappearing completely, the increase in awareness about the problem may yet pull the lake back from the brink of total environmental disaster."*
   B. *"Until recently, the Aral Sea was one of the largest lakes in the world."*
   C. *"This massive irrigation project robbed the Aral Sea of its main sources of water."*
   D. *"In addition, a rapidly increasing population in the region put an even greater strain on the lake as the area's main water supply."*

10. Based on its usage in the fourth paragraph, which of the following is closest in meaning to the word *reclaim*?

   A. *prove ownership to*          B. *make useful again*

   C. *demand possession of*        D. *adjust the angle of*

 ## Soapbox Race

The first year that Daisy participated in the soapbox car race, her homemade car fell apart halfway down the hill. But she was so proud of that car. She had built it herself from an orange crate, an old plank she'd found at the dump, and a set of wheels she had taken off her skateboard. She had painted the car with her favorite colors, blue and gold. But it was her first time building anything, and as she picked up speed going down the hill, the vibration shook the orange crate loose from the plank. Before she knew it, she was lying on her side in the crate, watching the rest of her car bounce wildly down the hill. The crowd let out a sigh of disappointment as Daisy made the long walk down the hill to pick up the remnants of her race car.

The next year, when she told her father she wanted to race again, he looked doubtful. "Are you sure?" he asked. "I just don't want you to be disappointed again. And I don't want you to endanger yourself."

But Daisy was sure. Her father often called her "the little mule," because when she decided to do something, there was no way to change her mind. This time she made her racer out of an old metal wagon. She put larger wheels on it and made sure that everything was put together solidly so that it wouldn't shake apart during the race. Still, she was nervous. When it was her turn to race, she cautiously approached the starting line and gave her car a gentle push before hopping in. As she started down the hill, she could tell this racer was going much faster than the last one she'd built. The ride felt like butter compared to her last bumpy trip. But halfway down the hill, she once again ran into a problem. She was moving fast enough, but the car was drifting to the left and she couldn't steer it back toward the center of the road. She leaned to the right with all her might, but the car kept drifting left, finally crashing into the hay bales that lined the side of the race course. Again the crowd sighed with disappointment as her dreams of finishing the race vanished.

The next year, Daisy thought about skipping the soapbox car race. "You do whatever makes you happy," her father said.

But when Daisy thought some more, she realized that finally finishing the soapbox car race would definitely make her happy. She designed a new soapbox car from scratch, cutting the chassis and seat from sturdy wood with the help of her older brother. She added a steering wheel that connected to the front wheels so she could keep her car on course. She also made a bullet-shaped cone for the front to make her car less resistant to wind.

When Daisy started down the hill in her new soapbox racer, she could tell she was moving faster than ever before. She held tight to the steering wheel, making sure to keep the car on course. She could hear the cheers and claps from spectators along the side of the road as she raced down the hill. When she reached the bottom, she was moving so fast that she was afraid she might never slow down. She pulled hard on the brake and finally came to a stop amid the cheering crowd that had gathered at the finish line.

Daisy was thrilled that she finally completed the race. It took three years, but she had accomplished her goal. Her father ran up to her, beaming with pride. "You are a remarkable young woman," he said, and hugged her. Everyone around them began to cheer.

"I'm so happy I was finally able to finish," Daisy said.

"Finish?" said her father. "Daisy, you won the race. You were the fastest by five seconds!"

# ❓ Questions

11. What is the main theme of the story? Support your answer with details from the story.

_____

_____

_____

_____

12. Based on its usage in the second paragraph, which of the following is closest in meaning to the word *endanger*?
    A. *disappoint*
    C. *remove from danger*
    B. *disobey rules*
    D. *put at risk*

13. According to the passage, how many soapbox race cars did Daisy build before she won?
    A. *one*
    C. *three*
    B. *two*
    D. *four*

14. How does Daisy's father's attitude about the race compare with Daisy's attitude about the race?

_____

_____

_____

_____

15. Why does Daisy's father call her "the little mule"?

_____

_____

_____

_____

16. Based on its usage in the third paragraph, which of the following is closest in meaning to the word *cautiously*?
    A. *with great excitement*
    C. *with great speed*
    B. *with great care*
    D. *with great noise*

17. How does Daisy respond to the challenges she faces in the story?
    A. *She gives up.*
    B. *She asks her father for help.*
    C. *She keeps trying with the same type of racer.*
    D. *She keeps trying, but with a different type of racer.*

18. In the fourth paragraph, what does it mean that Daisy's ride "felt like butter"?
    A. *It was smooth.*          B. *It was slippery.*
    C. *It was sluggish.*        D. *It was yellow.*

19. Based on its usage in the sixth paragraph, which of the following is closest in meaning to the word *spectators*?
    A. *binoculars*              B. *contestants*
    C. *onlookers*               D. *judges*

20. What is your opinion of Daisy as a person?

    _____

    _____

    _____

 **Read the paragraph and decide on the best word to fill each blank.**

(1) _____ the big football game, Jacob asked me which team I was rooting for. (2) I _____ about it all week, and finally I decided that I would root for the Wolverines. (3) _____, I still hoped the Pelicans would play well and offered up a real challenge. (4) On game day, I _____ to Jacob's house to watch the game on his family's large-screen television. (5) Jacob's mother surprised me by announcing, "You are welcome at our house any time. But you do _____ that you've entered Pelican territory, don't you?"

21. In sentence 1, which word is the best choice to fill the blank?
    A. *Past*                    B. *Along*
    C. *Over*                    D. *Before*

22. In sentence 2, which word is the best choice to fill the blank?
    A. *am thinking*
    B. *has been thinking*
    C. *had been thinking*
    D. *were thinking*

23. In sentence 3, which word is the best choice to fill the blank?
    A. *However*                 B. *Also*
    C. *In particular*           D. *Therefore*

24. In sentence 4, which word is the best choice to fill the blank?
    A. *gone*                          B. *went*
    C. *has been going*                D. *were going*

25. In sentence 5, which word is the best choice to fill the blank?
    A. *knowed*                        B. *known*
    C. *knew*                          D. *know*

26. Read this draft of a paragraph. Correct the grammar, punctuation, spelling, and capitalization.

Living in a part of the country with sunny sumers and snowy winters is better then living wear the whether is alway the same many people who lives in warm climates can't understand how a person can put up with the cold and snow that winter brings. But if you've lived in a place like this most of your life, it does'nt bother you. in fact, each year you look forward to the for seasons—the snow of winter, the mild breezes of spring, the warm days of summer, and the beautiful colors of autum leaves. In my opinion, living in a place with varying seasons make life more interesting and enjoyable.

_____

_____

_____

_____

_____

_____

_____

_____

_____

_____

 **Answer Key**

Note: The answers to open-ended, constructed response questions are sample answers. Answers will vary, but look for the main ideas to be included.

Highlight any questions that your child gets wrong. Looking at the wrong answers may help to reveal one or more standards with which your child is struggling. Even if your child has done well on this pre-test, reviewing the lessons will help him or her become a better reader and writer.

| Passage | Question | Answer | Standard(s) |
|---|---|---|---|
| The Aral Sea | 1 | The Aral Sea was once very large, but humans have caused it to shrink greatly. | RI.5.2 |
| | 2 | C | RI.5.1 |
| | 3 | A | RI.5.4 |
| | 4 | Soviet engineers took water headed for the Aral Sea and used it for crops. | RI.5.2 |
| | 5 | D | RI.5.1 |
| | 6 | C | RI.5.4 |
| | 7 | B | RI.5.8 |
| | 8 | D | RI.5.4 |
| | 9 | A | RI.5.8 |
| | 10 | B | RI.5.4 |
| Soapbox Race | 11 | The main theme is to not give up on your goal. Daisy kept trying to built a soapbox that was good enough to help her finish the race. After three tries, she not only finished the race but actually won it. | RL.5.2 |
| | 12 | D | RL.5.4 |
| | 13 | C | RL.5.1 |
| | 14 | Daisy's father is worried about how disappointed Daisy feels each time she tries to compete. He supports her wishes to try again and again, but it would be ok with him if she decided to give up. Daisy, on the other hand, is much more focused on her goal. She isn't that concerned about how disappointed she might feel if she continues to lose. | RL.5.3 |
| | 15 | Daisy's father calls her "the little mule" because mules are known for being stubborn. In a way, Daisy is stubborn because she doesn't give up trying to reach her goal. | RL.5.1 |
| | 16 | B | RL.5.4 |
| | 17 | D | RL.5.2 |
| | 18 | A | RL.5.4 |
| | 19 | C | RL.5.4 |
| | 20 | Answers will vary but should be well-supported by details from the story. Daisy is a very persistent girl. She makes up her mind to try to finish the soapbox race, and makes three tries over three different years. In my opinion, three years is too long to continue to want the same goal. Still, you have to admire her for finally achieving her goal. | RL.5.1, W.5.1 |
| | 21 | D | W.5.5 |
| | 22 | C | W.5.5 |
| | 23 | A | W.5.5 |
| | 24 | B | W.5.5 |
| | 25 | D | W.5.5 |
| | 26 | Living in a part of the country with sunny summers and snowy winters is better than living where the weather is always the same. Many people who live in warm climates can't understand how a person can put up with the cold and snow that winter brings. But if you've lived in a place like this most of your life, it doesn't bother you. In fact, each year you look forward to the four seasons—the snow of winter, the mild breezes of spring, the warm days of summer, and the beautiful colors of autumn leaves. In my opinion, living in a place with varying seasons makes life more interesting and enjoyable. | W.5.1 |

# MATHEMATICS PRE-TEST

1. Use the area model to find the area of a rectangle with the dimensions $\frac{2}{3} \times \frac{5}{6}$.

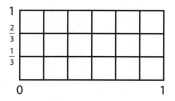

2. Which of the following is the best estimate for the quotient of 6,027 ÷ 118?
   *A.* 5
   *C.* 51.08
   *B.* 50
   *D.* 60

3. Which of the following shows 873.566 rounded to the nearest hundredth?
   *A.* 900
   *C.* 873.560
   *B.* 873.600
   *D.* 873.570

4. A public park has 896 flower bulbs. They want to plant them equally in 8 flower beds. How many bulbs should go in each flower bed? Show your work.

5. To make his favorite fruit punch recipe, Richard mixes $\frac{1}{2}$ gallon of apple juice, 1 pint of lemonade, 1 quart of grape juice, and 1 cup of water. How many cups of fruit punch will he have all together?

6. In the number 645.148, how much larger is the first 4 than the second 4?
   *A.* 10 times
   *C.* 1,000 times
   *B.* 100 times
   *D.* 10,000 times

7. Use an area model to solve 3,616 ÷ 8.

8. A shoebox can hold 5 rows of 8 one-inch cubes in the bottom of the box. 4 of these cubes stack up to match the height of the box. How many one-inch cubes could fill the entire box?

9. Which of the following is the correct solution for $135.8 + 24.2 = ?$
   A. 159.10                     B. 160
   C. 375.10                     D. 376.0

10. What is the volume of the figure shown below?

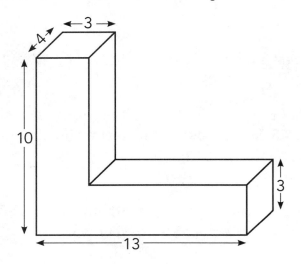

11. Which of the following is the correct solution for $8.2 \times 3.1 = ?$
    A. 24.142                    B. 24.2
    C. 24.16                     D. 25.42

12. What is $\frac{1}{5} \div 3$? Use a fraction bar to solve this problem.

13. Use a visual model to solve $\frac{1}{2} + \frac{1}{3} = ?$

14. Complete the area model to find $768 \div 6 = ?$

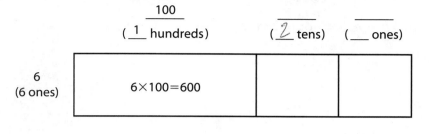

15. Use a number line to multiply $4 \times \dfrac{4}{5}$.

16. What is $395 \div 100$?

    A.  3.95                    B.  39.5
    C.  3,950                   D.  39,500

17. What is $6.4 \div 1.6$?

18. There are 18 students in Mr. Green's class. $\dfrac{2}{3}$ of the students are girls. How many girls are in Mr. Green's class?

    A.  9 girls                 B.  12 girls
    C.  6 girls                 D.  15 girls

19. What is $855 \div 19$?

20. Which of the following questions could be solved by multiplying $\dfrac{3}{4} \times 24$?

    A.  What is the final price of a $24 item on sale at $\dfrac{3}{4}$ of its original price?

    B.  Kimberly uses $\dfrac{3}{4}$ of a cup of flour to make one mini-cake. How much sugar would she need to make 24 mini-cakes?

    C.  There are 24 students in the class and $\dfrac{3}{4}$ of the students in a class are going on a field trip. How many are going on the field trip?

    D.  All of these

21. Sonya is framing a picture and needs to buy a piece of glass that is $\frac{4}{5}$ foot tall and $2\frac{1}{3}$ foot wide. Complete the area model below to determine the total area of the piece of glass she needs.

22. Which of the following is closest to the difference of $1\frac{3}{10}-\frac{3}{8}$?

    A. 0          B. $\frac{1}{2}$          C. 1          D. $1\frac{1}{2}$

23. Which of the following best approximates the product $25\times\frac{3}{8}$?

    A. 5          B. 75          C. 12          D. $12\frac{1}{2}$

24. The varsity basketball team, the junior-varsity basketball team, and the band are going to an away game. The school is providing coolers and paper cups for drinking water. The school calculated it should send 2.5 paper cups per person. If there are 9 members on the varsity team, 12 members on the junior-varsity team, and 17 members in the band, how many cups should the school send?

25. Which is the correct quotient of $8\div\frac{1}{4}$?

    A. $\frac{1}{32}$          B. $\frac{1}{2}$          C. 2          D. 32

# ✓ Answer Key

| Question | Answer | Explanation | Standard |
|---|---|---|---|
| 1 | $\dfrac{10}{18}$ or $\dfrac{5}{9}$. | | 5.NF.B.4, 5.NF.B.4a, 5.NF.B.4b |
| 2 | B | Choice A is off by a place value. Choice C is not an estimate—it is the exact quotient, rounded to the nearest hundredth. Estimating is about quickly getting close to the answer, rather than rounding. Choice C is off by 10, and may be the result of only considering the first digit of each number. | 5.NBT.B.6 |
| 3 | D | Choice A is rounded to the nearest hundred. Choice B is rounded to the nearest tenth. Choice C is incorrectly rounded down instead of up. | 5.NBT.A.4 |
| 4 | 112 | | 5.NBT.B.6 |
| 5 | 15 cups | First convert all quantities to the same unit of measure—cups are easiest, since they are smallest. ½ gallon is 8 cups. 1 pint is 2 cups, 1 quart is 4 cups. The water added is already in the correct units (1 cup), So altogether, he is mixing 8 + 2 + 42 + 1 cups, which is 53 cups of fruit punch. | 5.NF.A.2, 5.NF.A.1 |
| 6 | C | The 4s are 3 place values apart, so to get from one to the other, you would multiply by 10 three times: $10 \times 10 \times 10 = 1{,}000$ | 5.NBT.A.1 |
| 7 | 452 | | 5.NBT.B.6 |
| 8 | 160 | The area of the base of the box is $5 \times 8 = 40$ square inches, and the height is 4. The volume is $40 \times 4 = 160$ cubic inches. | 5.MD.C.5c |
| 9 | B | 8 tenths plus 2 tenths makes 1 whole, which is added to the sum of 135 and 24. $135 + 24 = 159$, and $159 + 1 = 160$. | 5.NBT.B.7 |

| Question | Answer | Explanation | Standard |
|---|---|---|---|
| 10 | 240 cubic inches | The shape can be cut into two rectangular prisms, as shown below. The volume of the upper prism is $4 \times 3 \times 7 = 84$ cubic units, and the volume of the lower prism is $4 \times 13 \times 3 = 156$ cubic units. The total is $84 + 156 = 240$ cubic units. | 5.MD.C.5c |

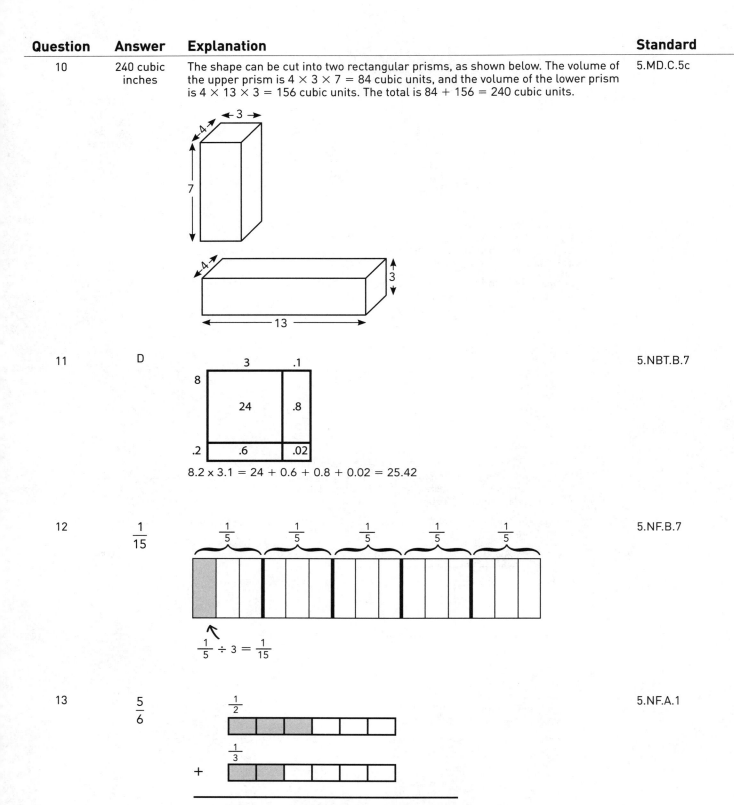

| Question | Answer | Explanation | Standard |
|---|---|---|---|
| 11 | D | $8.2 \times 3.1 = 24 + 0.6 + 0.8 + 0.02 = 25.42$ | 5.NBT.B.7 |
| 12 | $\frac{1}{15}$ | $\frac{1}{5} \div 3 = \frac{1}{15}$ | 5.NF.B.7 |
| 13 | $\frac{5}{6}$ | | 5.NF.A.1 |

| Question | Answer | Explanation | Standard |
|---|---|---|---|
| 14 | 128 | | 5.NBT.B.6 |

$$\underline{100} \qquad \underline{20} \qquad \underline{8}$$
$$(\underline{1}\ \text{hundreds}) \quad (\underline{2}\ \text{tens}) \quad (\underline{8}\ \text{ones})$$

| 6<br>(6 ones) | $6\times100=600$ | $6\times20=120$ | $6\times8=48$ |
|---|---|---|---|

| 15 | $3\frac{1}{5}$ | | 5.NF.B.4 |

| 16 | A | When dividing by a power of 10 (10, 100, 1,000, etc.), the place value of each digit becomes smaller. Since we are dividing by 100, each digit's place value becomes smaller by 2 places. | 5.NBT.B.6 |

| 17 | 4 | The quotient is 4. Use a number line model, as shown below: | 5.NBT.B.7 |

| 18 | B | | 5.NF.B.4,<br>5.NF.B.4a,<br>5.NF.B.6 |

$$\frac{2}{3}\ \text{are girls} \qquad \frac{1}{3}\ \text{are boys}$$

| 19 | 45 | | 5.NBT.B.6 |

$$19\ \overline{)855}$$
$$\underline{-760}\ \big|\ 40$$
$$95$$
$$\underline{-95}\ \big|\ 5$$
$$0$$

| 20 | D | Every question could be answered by multiplying $\frac{3}{4}\times24$. | 5.NF.B.4,<br>5.NF.B.4a |

| 21 | $1\frac{13}{15}$ | | 5.NF.B.4,<br>5.NF.B.4a,<br>5.NF.B.4b,<br>5.NF.B.6 |

| 22 | C | $1\frac{3}{10}$ is close to $1\frac{1}{2}$ and $\frac{3}{8}$ is close to $\frac{1}{2}$, so their difference will be close to 1. | 5.NF.A.1 |

| Question | Answer | Explanation | Standard |
|---|---|---|---|
| 23 | C | $\frac{3}{8}$ is a little bit less than $\frac{1}{2}$, so the product will be around half of 25, which is $12\frac{1}{2}$. | 5.NF.B.4, 5.NF.B.4a |
| 24 | 95 cups | The school should send $9 + 12 + 17 = 38$. Multiplying this by 2.5 will give the number of cups and $38 \times 2.5 = 95$ cups. | 5.NBT.B.7 |
| 25 | D | $8 \div \frac{1}{4}$ asks how many times $\frac{1}{4}$ can fit into 8. Since $\frac{1}{4}$ fits in 1 whole 4 times, it would take a total of $4 \times 8 = 32$ pieces to make up 8 wholes. | 5.NF.B.7 |

# IV

# OVERVIEW

For Grade 5, the ELA Common Core Standards focus on main ideas and how they are presented. For informational texts, this means identifying the main idea of the passage. The standards also require students to identify and analyze arguments by looking at the reasons and evidence presented by the author. For literary passages, students are expected to be able to identify the theme, and to identify and describe story elements such as character, setting, and events. For writing, students are expected to write opinion pieces that make effective use of arguments, and use planning and revising to help create stronger writing.

Listed below are the ELA Common Core Standards for Grade 5 that we have identified as "power standards." We consider these standards to be critical for your child's success. Each lesson focuses on a single power standard so that you and your child may practice to achieve mastery. The applicable standards are divided into three categories: Reading—Informational Text; Reading—Literature; and Writing.

## Reading—Informational Text

*CCSS.ELA-Literacy.RI.5.1:* Quote accurately from a text when explaining what the text says explicitly and when drawing inferences from the text.

*CCSS.ELA-Literacy.RI.5.2:* Determine two or more main ideas of a text and explain how they are supported by key details; summarize the text.

*CCSS.ELA-Literacy.RI.5.4:* Determine the meaning of general academic and domain-specific words and phrases in a text relevant to a *grade 5 topic or subject area*.

*CCSS.ELA-Literacy.RI.5.8:* Explain how an author uses reasons and evidence to support particular points in a text, identifying which reasons and evidence support which point(s).

## Reading—Literature

*CCSS.ELA-Literacy.RL.5.1:* Quote accurately from a text when explaining what the text says explicitly and when drawing inferences from the text.

*CCSS.ELA-Literacy.RL.5.2:* Determine a theme of a story, drama, or poem from details in the text, including how characters in a story or drama respond to challenges or how the speaker in a poem reflects upon a topic; summarize the text.

*CCSS.ELA-Literacy.RL.5.3:* Compare and contrast two or more characters, settings, or events in a story or drama, drawing on specific details in the text (e.g., how characters interact).

*CCSS.ELA-Literacy.RL.5.4:* Determine the meaning of words and phrases as they are used in a text, including figurative language such as metaphors and similes.

## Writing

*CCSS.ELA-Literacy.W.5.1:* Write opinion pieces on topics or texts, supporting a point of view with reasons and information.

*CCSS.ELA-Literacy.W.5.5:* With guidance and support from peers and adults, develop and strengthen writing as needed by planning, revising, editing, rewriting, or trying a new approach.

# READING

For the reading standards, Common Core breaks texts into two basic types: (1) Informational Texts, which essentially cover all types of nonfiction; and (2) Literature, which includes stories, drama, and poetry. The following chart is from the Common Core Standards Initiative website provides a brief overview of the range of text types. For the purposes of assessment, texts are also selected from a broad range of cultures and time periods.

| Literature | | | Informational Text |
|---|---|---|---|
| Stories | Dramas | Poetry | Literary Nonfiction and Historical, Scientific, and Technical Texts |
| Includes children's adventure stories, folktales, legends, fables, fantasy, realistic fiction, and myth | Includes staged dialogue and brief familiar scenes | Includes nursery rhymes and the subgenres of the narrative poem, limerick, and free verse poem | Includes biographies and autobiographies; books about history, social studies, science, and the arts; technical texts, including directions, forms, and information displayed in graphs, charts, or maps; and digital sources on a range of topics |

As practice is the best way to build reading skills, encourage your child to read a variety of literary works and informational texts.

## Informational Text

Informational texts include literary nonfiction, such as biographies or memoirs, as well as historical, scientific, and technical texts. They include expository, persuasive, and functional texts in the form of personal essays, opinion pieces, speeches, essays, journalism, and other nonfiction accounts. A variety of types of informational texts are included in this section to give your child practice across a range of genres and subgenres.

## Literature

The literature category for grades K-5 includes three main subcategories: stories, dramas, and poetry. Stories may be adventure stories, realistic fiction, folktales and fables, legends and myths, and fantasy. Dramas include the written text that would be used for a play, with dialogue, stage directions, and scenes. Poetry includes nursery rhymes, narrative poems, limericks, and free verse. A variety of stories is included in this section of the book to give your child practice with the genre used most commonly on tests. Because practice is the best way to build reading skills, encourage your child to read a variety of literary works.

# WRITING

The Common Core Standards for writing are tied closely to reading, since many of the skills your child learns to read effectively are also applicable to their own writing. In general, your child will be asked to write short passages that express a specific viewpoint or support a specific argument. For these writing passages, the emphasis will be on using information, details, and examples to support the main idea or ideas. Your child will also be expected to create writing that flows smoothly, with an introductory sentence or paragraph, a main body, and a closing sentence or paragraph. In addition to writing an effective draft, your child will also be asked to revise, adjust, and improve their own writing and the writing of others.

Another element that is critical to your child's writing skills is mastery of basic grammar and mechanics appropriate for his or her grade level. This is shown through your child's own writing, as well as through revising and improving the writing of others.

# THE STANDARD

**RI.5.1:** *Quotes and Inferences – Informational Text*
*Quote accurately from a text when explaining what the text says explicitly and when drawing inferences from the text.*

## What does it mean?

This informational text standard focuses on a child's ability to use accurate quotes when explaining what is stated or suggested in a text.

## Try this together

Here's a brief passage about cuttlefish that is similar to the kinds of passages used to test this standard. To address this reading standard, a teacher might ask questions such as the ones that follow the passage, or assign them as homework. We have provided possible answers in the "Answers" section, along with an explanation of how the questions connect to the standard.

Before trying this exercise with your child, read through the passage and the questions that follow it yourself. Then have your child read the passage aloud to you and the answer the questions that follow. Talk about the answers together. Help your child notice how he or she can find answers to questions by looking back at the passage.

## The Cuttlefish

The cuttlefish is a strange creature related to the octopus and squid. Some people even mistake cuttlefish for squid. Like squid, they have eight arms and two longer tentacles. They also squirt ink as a defense mechanism if they are in danger. However, cuttlefish have some other features that are unique to their order.

The cuttlefish contains a bony internal structure called a cuttlebone that runs most of the length of its body. Despite the name, the cuttlebone is not actually made of bone. It is made of aragonite, a natural calcium carbonate material. The cuttlebone is filled with tiny pockets that can trap gas. This can be used by the cuttlefish to become more or less buoyant, allowing the creature to move up and down through the water. If you have a pet bird, you may have seen a cuttlebone before. They are often used as a chew snack and calcium supplement for birds.

The most notable feature about the cuttlefish is its ability to change its skin color. Like a chameleon, the cuttlefish can quickly transform the color of its skin to match its environment. The skin of a cuttlefish contains cell parts known as chromatophores. The chromatophores come in different colors, and the cuttlefish can control which of these colored elements are visible. By showing only colors that match its surroundings, a cuttlefish can camouflage itself to avoid being eaten by other animals. A cuttlefish can completely change its color and pattern in about a second.

Cuttlefish were once caught for their reddish-brown ink, which was called sepia and used by ancient Greeks and Romans for writing. Now, cuttlefish are caught mainly for food. Their ink is used in certain dishes, giving sauce or pasta a rich dark color.

## ? Questions

Make sure to use accurate quotes to answer each question.

1. Which two sentences describe how cuttlefish are similar to squid?

_____

_____

_____

_____

2. Which sentence details how a cuttlefish uses its cuttlebone?

_____

_____

3. Which phrase does the author use to describe the cuttlefish's most notable feature?

_____

_____

_____

_____

4. What part of a cuttlefish's skin allows it to change color?

_____

_____

_____

_____

5. Which sentence suggests that cuttlefish are no longer caught mainly to make writing ink?

_____

_____

_____

_____

# ☑ Answers

1. Which two sentences describe how cuttlefish are similar to squid?

   *"Like squid, they have eight arms and two longer tentacles. They also squirt ink as a defense mechanism." This question requires students to recognize the comparison that the passage makes between the two animals.*

2. Which sentence details how a cuttlefish uses its cuttlebone?

   *"This can be used by the cuttlefish to become more or less buoyant, allowing the creature to move up and down through the water." This question requires students to find the sentence that addresses the importance of the cuttlebone.*

3. Which phrase does the author use to describe the cuttlefish's most notable feature?

   *"its ability to change its skin color." In this question, students must draw inferences from the passage as they respond to the question.*

4. What part of a cuttlefish's skin allows it to change color?

   *"cell parts known as chromatophores." This question builds on the previous question, requiring students to locate the specific detail that applies to the cuttlefish's color change.*

5. Which sentence suggests that cuttlefish are no longer caught mainly to make writing ink?

   *"Now, cuttlefish are caught mainly for food." In this question, students must draw inferences from the passage as they respond to the question.*

# Extra practice

To help your child work on the skills assessed by this standard, try this activity:

1. Find a library or online resource containing a short article on an interesting subject.
2. Read through the article with your child. Then ask your child to write a summary of the article, including five quotes from the original article. Make sure the quotes your child includes are accurate, and make sure your child mentions where the quotes are taken from.

Through this activity your child will be directly practicing the skills listed in the standard. She will quote specific text containing details and information related to the main topic of a passage.

# Quiz

Have your child read this passage and write the answers independently in the space provided.

## READ *The Story of Mankind* by Hendrik Willem van Loon (excerpt)

Soon central Europe was dotted with small principalities, each one ruled by a duke or a count or a baron or a bishop, as the case might be, and organised as a fighting unit. These dukes and counts and barons had sworn to be faithful to the king who had given them their "feudum" (hence our word "feudal,") in return for their loyal services and a certain amount of taxes. But travel in those days was slow and the means of communication were exceedingly poor. The royal or imperial administrators therefore enjoyed great independence, and within the boundaries of their own province they assumed most of the rights, which in truth belonged to the king.

But you would make a mistake if you supposed that the people of the eleventh century objected to this form of government. They supported Feudalism because it was a very practical and necessary institution. Their Lord and Master usually lived in a big stone house erected on the top of a steep rock or built between deep moats, but within sight of his subjects. In case of danger the subjects found shelter behind the walls of the baronial stronghold. That is why they tried to live as near the castle as possible and it accounts for the many European cities, which began their career around a feudal fortress.

But the knight of the early middle ages was much more than a professional soldier. He was the civil servant of that day. He was the judge of his community and he was the chief of police. He caught the highwaymen and protected the wandering pedlars who were the merchants of the eleventh century. He looked after the dikes so that the countryside should not be flooded (just as the first noblemen had done in the valley of the Nile four thousand years before). He encouraged the Troubadours who wandered from place to place telling the stories of the ancient heroes who had fought in the great wars of the migrations. Besides, he protected the churches and the monasteries within his territory, and although he could neither read nor write, (it was considered unmanly to know such things,) he employed a number of priests who kept his accounts and who registered the marriages and the births and the deaths which occurred within the baronial or ducal domains.

# Questions

1. According to the passage, which of the following people did NOT rule a principality under feudalism?

   *A. a duke*      *B. a merchant*      *C. a baron*      *D. a count*

2. What phrase describes what happened as a result of slow travel and poor communication in feudal times?

   *A. "The royal or imperial administrators therefore enjoyed great independence"*
   *B. "dukes and counts and barons had sworn to be faithful to the king"*
   *C. "they tried to live as near the castle as possible"*
   *D. "the knight of the early middle ages was much more than a professional soldier"*

3.  According to the passage, what did people do when there was danger in their feudal town?
    A.  *"protected the churches and the monasteries within his territory"*
    B.  *"They supported Feudalism because it was a very practical and necessary institution."*
    C.  *"encouraged the Troubadours who wandered from place to place"*
    D.  *"the subjects found shelter behind the walls of the baronial stronghold"*

4.  Which of the following best describes a Troubadour?
    A.  *a judge*                            B.  *a travelling storyteller*
    C.  *a priest*                           D.  *a war hero*

5.  Which phrase describes why the knights couldn't read or write?
    A.  *"he was the chief of police"*
    B.  *"they assumed most of the rights which in truth belonged to the king"*
    C.  *"it was considered unmanly to know such things"*
    D.  *"they tried to live as near the castle as possible"*

# ✓ Answers

1.  *According to the passage, which of the following people did NOT rule a principality under feudalism?*

    *The correct answer is B. Your child should note that the first paragraph states, "central Europe was dotted with small principalities, each one ruled by a duke or a count or a baron." This response requires an accurate quote from the passage.*

2.  What phrase describes what happened as a result of slow travel and poor communication in feudal times?

    *The correct answer is A. Because travel was slow and communication poor in feudal times, the feudal lords had independence and could do things that the king normally would. This response requires an accurate quote from the passage.*

3.  According to the passage, what did people do when there was danger in their feudal town?

    *The correct answer is D. Your child should note that the second paragraph describes how the feudal lord lived in a large stone house on high ground or surrounded by a moat. The common people went there for protection in times of danger. This response requires an accurate quote from the passage.*

4.  Which of the following best describes a Troubadour?

    *The correct answer is B. The third paragraph describes Troubadours as people who "wandered from place to place telling the stories of the ancient heroes who had fought in the great wars of the migrations." This response requires an accurate quote from the passage.*

5.  Which phrase describes why the knights couldn't read or write?

    *The correct answer is C. The third paragraph mentions that knights could not read or write because "it was considered unmanly to know such things." This response requires an accurate quote from the passage.*

# THE STANDARD

*RI.5.2: Main Idea and Key Details – Informational Text*
*Determine two or more main ideas of a text and explain how they are supported by key details; summarize the text.*

## What does it mean?

This informational text standard focuses on a child's ability to identify the main ideas of a passage, to recognize details that support each main idea, and to summarize a passage.

## Try this together

Here's a brief passage about expansion across the American West that is similar to the kinds of passages used to test this standard. To address this reading standard, a teacher might ask questions such as the ones that follow the passage, or assign them as homework. We have provided possible answers in the "Answers" section, along with an explanation of how the questions connect to the standard.

Before trying this exercise with your child, read through the passage and the questions that follow it yourself. Then have your child read the passage aloud to you and answer the questions that follow. Talk about the answers together. Help your child notice how he or she can find answers to questions by looking back at the passage.

## Inventions and the American West

The expansion of the American West owes a huge debt to one person: John Deere. Deere was a blacksmith born in Vermont in 1804. He later moved to Illinois, which was then considered the frontier of the American West. He put his blacksmith skills to use by creating plows for farmers. Most plows at the time were made from cast iron, which was heavy and durable. These plows were well-suited to eastern soil, but the sticky clay soil of the midwest clung to the iron plows. This meant that the operator had to stop working and clean the soil from the plow frequently.

Deere's great innovation was to use steel instead of cast iron for the cutting edge, or share, of the plow. The steel plow cut through the sticky frontier soil with ease. Another of Deere's refinements was a curved moldboard, which turned over the soil as it was plowed. This helped bring nutrients in the soil up to the surface, which helped crops grow. Deere's invention became wildly successful and allowed farmers to take advantage of the wide-open frontier spaces of the American West.

However, there was another invention that was even more instrumental in the nation's expansion westward. As settlers continued west beyond the Mississippi River, they needed a way to transport crops and goods back and forth from the east. Wagon trains were an early form of transport, but they were slow and limited in capacity. Fortunately, the steam locomotive rose to the challenge. Steam locomotives could move much faster and carry much more than wagons. By the 1820s, steam railways were already in operation in England. The first U.S. steam locomotive was the Tom Thumb, built for the Baltimore and Ohio Railroad in 1829. The railroad network quickly expanded during the 1830s and 1840s, moving farther westward. But it was not until the 1860s that a concerted effort was made to span the continent with rail. In 1869, the First Transcontinental Railroad began service, connecting California with an already established railroad network in Council Bluffs, Iowa. The steam locomotive quickly became the primary mode of transportation for people and goods traveling across the United States.

# Questions

1. What is the main idea of the first two paragraphs?

   _____

   _____

   _____

   _____

2. What is the main idea of the third paragraph?

   _____

   _____

   _____

3. What details explain how John Deere's plow was better than previous plows?

   _____

   _____

   _____

4. What details explain the advantages of steam locomotives over wagon trains?

   _____

   _____

   _____

5. In your own words, write a short summary of the passage.

_____

_____

_____

_____

_____

_____

_____

 **Answers**

1. What is the main idea of the first two paragraphs?

   *Answers will vary but should include the include the idea that John Deere created a new kind of plow that allowed farmers to more easily farm soil in the American West. This question requires students to identify the main idea presented in the first half of the passage.*

2. What is the main idea of the third paragraph?

   *Answers will vary but should include the idea that the invention of the steam locomotive made it easier to transport people and goods across the United States. This question requires students to determine an entirely different main idea from the one they identified earlier in the passage.*

3. What details explain how John Deere's plow was better than previous plows?

   *Deere's plow was made of steel, which cut through the soil better. Also, Deere's plow had a curved moldboard that turned the soil as it plowed. This question requires students to locate important details that prove the idea that Deere improved the plow.*

4. What details explain the advantages of steam locomotives over wagon trains?

   *Steam locomotives were faster and could carry more than wagon trains. In this question, students must locate important details that prove the value of steam locomotives.*

5. In your own words, write a short summary of the passage.

   *Answers will vary, but an acceptable answer will include these important points: John Deere's plow made it easier for farmers to use the soil in the west; and steam locomotives made it easier to transport people and goods across the United States. This question requires students to summarize the most important ideas presented in the passage.*

# Extra practice

To help your child work on the skills assessed by this standard, try this activity:

1. Select a short news article from the newspaper or an online source.
2. Read the article aloud with your child.
3. Create a table on a sheet of paper containing six different cells. At the top of the first cell, write "Who?" At the top of the second cell, write "What?" At the top of the third cell, write "When?" At the top of the fourth cell, write "Where?" At the top of the fifth cell, write "Why?" At the top of the sixth cell, write "How?"
4. Ask your child to fill in each box with information from the article. For example, the first cell should identify who (person or topic) the article is about. The second cell should identify what is important about that person or topic. And so on.

Through this activity, your child will be directly practicing the skills covered by the standard. He or she will read and summarize an informational article using a special system to break down the information in a meaningful way.

## Quiz

Have your child read this passage and write the answers independently in the space provided.

## *American History Stories, Volume II* by Mara L. Pratt (excerpt)
## The Stamp Act

One of the first things England did to raise money from the colonists, was to issue the Stamp Act.

The king sent over a large amount of paper on which had been put a certain stamp. This paper the king ordered the colonists to use on all their government writing.

Nothing, so the king said, would be considered of any value unless it was written on this stamped paper. For example, suppose a man owed another man a hundred dollars. When he paid the debt, the receipt would not be considered of any value unless it was written on this particular paper. Suppose a young man and maiden were to go before the minister to be married; the marriage was not legal, so the king said, unless the minister did the writing, which was always given the married bride and groom, on this stamped paper.

Now, as the king had put a very high price upon this paper, you can see how, by compelling the American colonists to buy it, it was but one way of getting a heavy tax from them.

The colonists all over the country were furious when this stamped paper was sent to them.

The Boston people declared they wouldn't buy one sheet of it; they would buy nothing, sell nothing; the young men and maidens would not get married; they would do nothing, indeed, which should compel them to use this stamped paper.

# ❓ Questions

1. What is the main idea of this passage?
   A. *The King of England issued the Stamp Act.*
   B. *The Stamp Act was an unpopular method of taxation on the American colonies.*
   C. *Buying the special stamped paper was expensive.*
   D. *The American colonists did not like the King of England.*

2. Which of the following details from the passage does NOT describe a way that the Stamp Act would affect the colonists?
   A. *The Boston papermaking mills were no longer allowed to make paper.*
   B. *All receipts had to be used on stamped paper.*
   C. *Ministers had to write marriage licenses on stamped paper.*
   D. *Colonists had to pay more money for the stamped paper.*

3. Which of the following is a detail from the passage that describes the *main* reason why the colonists did not like the Stamp Act?
   A. *The Stamp Act prevented the colonists from getting married.*
   B. *All of the colonies' money had to be re-printed on stamped paper.*
   C. *The stamped paper was much more expensive than regular paper.*
   D. *The King didn't use the stamped paper himself.*

4. Which of the following is a detail from the passage that describes how the Boston colony reacted to the Stamp Act?
   A. *They continued writing receipts on unstamped paper.*
   B. *They refused to do anything that would require buying or using the stamped paper.*
   C. *They burned the stamped paper.*
   D. *They bought all of the stamped paper.*

5. Which of the following is the best summary of the passage?
   A. *The King of England tried to tax the American colonists with the Stamp Act, but the colonists were angered by it and refused to buy the stamped paper.*
   B. *The King of England needed to tax the American colonies because running them took a lot of money.*
   C. *The Boston colonists refused to do anything that needed stamped paper.*
   D. *There were many taxes that were imposed on the American colonies, and the Stamp Act was the worst one of all.*

# ✓ Answers

1. What is the main idea of this passage?

   *The correct answer is B. After reading the passage, your child should assess that this is the best explanation of the passage's main idea. The King of England issued the Stamp Act, and the colonists strongly opposed it.*

2. Which of the following details from the passage does NOT describe a way that the Stamp Act would affect the colonists?

   *The correct answer is A. This is the only detail that is not mentioned in the passage. The passage mentions nothing about papermaking mills in Boston.*

3. Which of the following is a detail from the passage that describes the *main* reason why the colonists did not like the Stamp Act?

   *The correct answer is C. The fourth paragraph says that the king "had put a very high price upon this paper," which meant that it was much more expensive than regular paper. By forcing the colonists to use this paper for certain things, it was like putting a tax on them.*

4. Which of the following is a detail from the passage that describes how the Boston colony reacted to the Stamp Act?

   *The correct answer is B. The sixth paragraph states that the Boston colonists, "would do nothing, indeed, which should compel them to use this stamped paper." Your child should note that the other details are not found in the passage.*

5. Which of the following is the best summary of the passage?

   *The correct answer is A. This is the best summary of the passage. Your child might recognize the other choices from the passage, but they do not represent the passage's main idea.*

# THE STANDARD

**RI.5.8:** *Analyzing an Argument – Informational Text*
*Explain how an author uses reasons and evidence to support particular points in a text, identifying which reasons and evidence support which point(s).*

## What does it mean?

This informational text standard focuses on a child's ability to figure out how an author uses reasons and evidence to support a particular argument or viewpoint presented in a passage.

## Try this together

Here's a brief passage about Japanese-American internment during World War II. It presents a specific argument or viewpoint on the issue. To address the reading standard, a teacher might ask questions such as the ones that follow the passage, or assign them as homework. We have provided possible answers in the "Answers" section, along with an explanation of how the questions connect to the standard.

Before trying this exercise with your child, read through the passage and the questions that follow it yourself. Then have your child read the passage aloud to you and the answer the questions. Talk about the answers together. Help your child notice how he or she can find answers to questions by looking back at the passage.

## READ  Japanese American Internment

The internment of Japanese Americans during World War II is a dark period in U.S. history that should not be forgotten. After Japan's attack on Pearl Harbor, Hawaii, in December 1941, many Americans called for Japanese people living in the United States to be expelled or imprisoned. (Hawaii was not a state at the time, but was considered a U.S. territory.) Between 1942 and 1946, over one hundred thousand people of Japanese ancestry in the United States were forced to relocate to internment camps. The majority of these were American citizens, including tens of thousands of children. The older internees, immigrants who were born in Japan but moved to the United States, were not legally allowed to become American citizens at that time.

The Japanese American internees were moved by force from the west coast, where many of them lived, to camps built in desolate inland areas. Some of these camps were located in Idaho,

Arizona, and Utah. For the most part, internees were not allowed to leave the camps. Several people were shot and killed when they tried to escape the camps. Although the internment was ordered by the president, and the internees were not called prisoners, most modern scholars agree that this constituted a massive violation of civil rights. Some internees were allowed to enlist in the United States military, and they left the camp to fight for the cause of freedom even as their own family members were effectively imprisoned back in America.

In many cases, the imprisoned Japanese American families lost their homes and businesses when they were placed in internment. As the war dragged on, some Japanese Americans were allowed to leave the camps, but only if they agreed to relocate to the eastern United States, where they had no friends, relatives, or other resources. The internment of Japanese Americans was carried out to prevent Japanese spies from operating in the United States. Throughout the course of World War II, only ten Americans were convicted of spying for Japan. None of these spies were of Japanese descent.

# Questions

1. Describe, in one sentence, the argument the author is making in this passage.

   _____

   _____

2. In the second paragraph, what reasons and evidence are presented to support the argument that internment was no different than imprisonment?

   _____

   _____

   _____

3. What reasons and evidence are presented that might support the idea that internment was not like imprisonment?

   _____

   _____

   _____

   _____

4. According to the third paragraph, what was the main reason given for the internment of Japanese Americans during World War II?

   _____

   _____

   _____

5. What evidence does the author present to argue that internment of Japanese Americans was not necessary or helpful?

_____

_____

_____

_____

 **Answers**

*1.* Describe, in one sentence, the argument the author is making in this passage.

*Answers will vary but should contain the basic elements provided in this sample answer: The author thinks that internment of Japanese Americans during World War II was legally and morally wrong, and that the internment did not help the war effort as was intended. This is another question that asks the student to find a reason given by the author in support of the opposing view. This question requires students to identify the overall argument or viewpoint of the author by looking at the evidence and reasons presented.*

*2.* In the second paragraph, what reasons and evidence are presented to support the argument that internment was no different than imprisonment?

*Reasons and evidence that support the argument include: They were moved forcibly to camps in desolate areas; they were not allowed to leave; some internees were shot while trying to escape. This question requires students to recognize specific evidence and reasons for one particular argument within the passage.*

*3.* What reasons and evidence are presented that might support the idea that internment was *not* like imprisonment?

*The student should identify at least some of the following evidence presented in the second paragraph: The internment came about as a direct order from the president; the internees were not called prisoners; and some internees were allowed to leave. This question is tricky, because it asks students to find reasons and evidence that do not support the author's main argument. Often, an author will list the reasons and evidence given to support an opposing view; this is done so the author can then refute the evidence, which may strengthen the author's own argument.*

*4.* According to the third paragraph, what was the main reason given for the internment of Japanese Americans during World War II?

*The main reason given for internment was to prevent people of Japanese descent from spying for Japan.*

5. What evidence does the author present to argue that internment of Japanese Americans was not necessary or helpful?

*Although the passage provides many reasons to explain how internment was unfair or harmful to Japanese Americans, the main evidence to support the argument that internment did not help the war effort is given at the end of the passage: No people of Japanese descent in the United States were convicted of spying during World War II. This question focuses on one specific element of the author's argument: that internment did not help the war effort. Much of the passage deals with other elements of the author's argument. This particular issue is addressed only at the end of the passage.*

# Extra practice

To help your child work on the skills assessed by this standard, try this activity:

1. Using the Internet, find the text of a famous persuasive speech or article. For example, a number of famous speeches can be found at The History Place Great Speeches Collection (http://www.historyplace.com/speeches/previous.htm). Choose a speech with a strong argument.

2. Read the speech aloud. Then ask your child to explain the argument the speaker was making.

3. With your child, look through the text of the speech and identify reasons and information that the speaker uses to support his or her argument.

Through this activity, your child will be directly practicing the skills covered by the standard. He or she will examine a work that expresses a certain viewpoint and will identify reasons and examples that the author uses to support that viewpoint.

## Quiz

Have your child read this passage and write the answers independently in the space provided.

## Zoos

Have you ever been to the zoo? Zoos have been around for hundreds of years and exist all over the world, and millions of people visit them every year. Some people think that zoos shouldn't exist because they aren't how animals naturally live in the wild. However, zoos are actually really positive places for animals and are important for animal conservation.

If your idea of a zoo is a place full of animals in cages, then you'd be mistaken. Most zoos now take pride in having naturalistic enclosures for animals that are modeled after their natural habitats. Tigers will play in a grassy yard, and birds will fly from tree to tree in an open-air aviary. One of the most important aspects of a zookeeper's job is making sure the animals they care for are happy and entertained every day. Zookeepers do this by providing enrichment, which is the process of stimulating natural behaviors through food and play.

Zoos are also places where important conservation work is completed. Many animals you see in the zoo are endangered, which means that there aren't many of them left in the wild due to loss of their natural habitat or other pressures. Almost every animal you see in a zoo was born in a zoo—practically no wild animals are captured for zoos anymore. This means that scientists and zookeepers can study and learn more about the animals at the zoo instead of searching for them in the wild. The information they learn here can be used to protect and save the animals that live in the wild.

# Questions

1. Which sentence describes the argument the author is making in this passage?
   A. *The author likes going to zoos and thinks everyone else should too.*
   B. *The author thinks that zoos are good places for animals and conservation research.*
   C. *The author doesn't think zoos are good for animals.*
   D. *The author thinks that zoos are good but that animals should no longer be taken from the wild to fill them.*

2. Which of the following is NOT given as evidence in the second paragraph to support the argument that zoos are positive places for animals to live?
   A. *The animals live in enclosures that are modeled after their natural habitats.*
   B. *Zookeepers provide enrichment to keep them happy and entertained.*
   C. *The zoo animals feel safe in their cages.*
   D. *Some zoos have open-air aviaries so the birds can fly.*

3. According to the third paragraph, what is the main reason given for having animals in zoos for conservation?
   A. *Scientists can learn more about endangered animals in the zoo instead of going into the wild to find them.*
   B. *Endangered animals can be saved by taking them out of their natural habitats and putting them into zoos.*
   C. *Zoos only house non-endangered animals.*
   D. *Conservation work can only happen in zoos.*

4. What additional information would help make the author's argument in the second paragraph stronger?
   A. *A description of some common types of enrichment.*
   B. *A list of the kinds of birds found in an open-air aviary.*
   C. *The names of some famous zookeepers.*
   D. *More examples of naturalistic enclosures.*

5. In the third paragraph, what does the author say is one cause of animals becoming endangered?
   A. lack of enrichment
   B. being caught for zoos
   C. non-naturalistic habitats
   D. habitat loss

 Answers

1. Which sentence describes the argument the author is making in this passage?

   *The correct answer is B. This sentence describes the author's argument. All of the details in the passage support this statement.*

2. Which of the following is NOT given as evidence in the second paragraph to support the argument that zoos are positive places for animals to live?

   *The correct answer is C. Your child should note that this is not stated in the second paragraph. The second paragraph actually refutes the idea that zoo animals are kept in cages at all.*

3. According to the third paragraph, what is the main reason given for having animals in zoos for conservation?

   *The correct answer is A. The third paragraph states that research done in zoos can help scientists help endangered animals in the wild. The information researchers learn from zoo animals is very important.*

4. What additional information would help make the author's argument in the second paragraph stronger?

   *The correct answer is A. The final sentence of the second paragraph mentions what enrichment is, but doesn't give any examples. Having examples of common types of enrichment would help students get a better idea of how enrichment helps keep zoo animals happy and entertained.*

5. In the third paragraph, what does the author say is one cause of animals becoming endangered?

   *The correct answer is D. The third paragraph says that some animals are endangered "due to loss of their natural habitat or other pressures." Your child should note that none of the other details are mentioned.*

# THE STANDARD

*RI.5.4: Vocabulary – Informational Text*
*Determine the meaning of general academic and domain-specific words or phrases in a text relevant to a grade 5 topic or subject area.*

## What does it mean?

This informational text standard focuses on a child's ability to understand vocabulary. The standard deals with general academic and domain-specific words and phrases. *General academic words,* sometimes called Tier 2 words, are more likely to appear in written texts than in speech. They can include subtle or precise ways to say relatively simple things. An example at the fifth-grade level might be *insightful* or *bright* in place of *smart.* General academic words can appear across many different types of texts, both informational and literary in nature.

In contrast, *domain-specific* words are specific to a field of study. They may introduce a new idea or concept within the text. Understanding these words often requires students to look for clues within the text itself. The passage about the cuttlefish included for standard RI.5.1, for instance, introduced students to the word *chromatophores.* Domain-specific words may also be part of a glossary or defined in a footnote.

This standard is related to other general vocabulary standards that are part of the Vocabulary Acquisition and Use section of Common Core Language skills. The standard is sometimes tested in connection with those other standards, which are included here for easy reference:

*L.5.4:* Determine or clarify the meaning of unknown and multiple-meaning word and phrases based on grade 5 reading and content, choosing flexibly from a range of strategies.

- *L.5.4.a:* Use context (e.g., cause/effect relationships and comparisons in text) as a clue to the meaning of a word or phrase.
- *L.5.4.b:* Use common, grade-appropriate Greek and Latin affixes and roots as clues to the meaning of a word (e.g., *photograph, photosynthesis*).
- *L.5.4.c:* Consult reference materials (e.g., dictionaries, glossaries, thesauruses), both print and digital, to find the pronunciation and determine or clarify the precise meaning of key words and phrases.

*L.5.5:* Demonstrate understanding of figurative language, word relationships, and nuances in word meanings.

- *L.5.5.a:* Interpret figurative language, including similes and metaphors, in context.
- *L.5.5.b:* Recognize and explain the meaning of common idioms, adages, and proverbs.
- *L.5.5.c:* Use the relationship between particular words (e.g., synonyms, antonyms, homographs) to better understand each of the words.

As you can see from the vocabulary-related standards, success in this area requires students to be able to decipher word meaning using the context in which it is used and knowledge of root words and affixes (prefixes and suffixes). Students also will need to recognize the figurative use of language. (Figurative language involves the use of words or phrases in a way that is not their literal, or dictionary, meaning.)

# Try this together

Here's a brief passage about a very exciting fossil find. To address this reading standard, a teacher might ask questions such as the ones that follow the passage, or assign them as homework. We have provided possible answers in the "Answers" section, along with an explanation of how the questions connect to the standard.

Before trying this exercise with your child, read through the passage and the questions that follow it yourself. Then have your child read the passage aloud to you and the answer the questions. Talk about the answers together. Help your child notice how she can find answers to questions by looking back at the passage.

 ## The Big Dig

The big news among local science fans is that a partial skeleton of a dinosaur known as Edmontosaurus was found on Mount Haddon. A group of hikers stumbled upon the fossil accidentally while climbing the mountain. The fossil is located near the top, on the eastern face. It is unusual for fossils to be found at such an altitude, but this can be explained by Mount Haddon's unusual formation. It is considered a thrust peak, meaning that it was thrust upward when two plates of the Earth's crust collided. Originally, when the fossil was first formed, it was much lower to the ground.

It is also true that fossils are seldom found in this area. Only a few have ever been recorded, with the last one being uncovered more than twenty years ago. That last fossil was a trilobite, a marine creature that was about three inches long. You can see why this Edmontosaurus fossil is big news!

A team of volunteers from the local university have agreed to help excavate the fossil. This process can take months, since dirt and debris must be removed slowly and carefully. It would be very easy for someone to accidentally throw out a piece of fossil, thinking it was simply a rock! After the fossil has been dug out, it will be transported from the summit of the mountain to a lab at the university. There, experts can study the fossil and work on assembling the pieces.

Edmontosaurus is most notable for its long flat snout, which resembles a duck's bill. These "duck-billed" dinosaurs lived about seventy million years ago. They could grow to be nearly forty feet in length. The fossil from Mount Haddon, however, looks like it came from a dinosaur about twenty-five feet long.

## ? Questions

1. Based on its usage in the first paragraph, which of the following is closest in meaning to the word "altitude"?
   A. time of day                    B. depth
   C. height                         D. big distance

2. Based on its usage in the second paragraph, which of the following is closest in meaning to the word "seldom"?
   A. rarely                         B. often
   C. never                          D. only

3. Based on its usage in the third paragraph, which of the following is closest in meaning to the word "excavate"?
   A. bury                           B. explore
   C. rebuild                        D. unearth

4. Based on its usage in the third paragraph, which of the following is closest in meaning to the word "summit"?
   A. top                            B. base
   C. rock                           D. side

5. Based on its usage in the fourth paragraph, which of the following is closest in meaning to the word "resembles"?
   A. evolves into
   B. looks like
   C. is larger than
   D. is smaller than

## ✓ Answers

1. Based on its usage in the first paragraph, which of the following is closest in meaning to the word "altitude"?
   The correct answer is C. In this passage, the word has the same meaning as "height." This question requires students to use context to determine the meaning of the word.

2. Based on its usage in the second paragraph, which of the following is closest in meaning to the word "seldom"?

*The correct answer is A. In this passage, the word has the same meaning as "rarely." This question also requires students to use context to determine the meaning of the word.*

3. Based on its usage in the third paragraph, which of the following is closest in meaning to the word "excavate"?

*The correct answer is D. In this passage, the word has the same meaning as "unearth." This question requires students to use context and knowledge of the Latin affix "ex" to determine the meaning of the word..*

4. Based on its usage in the fourth paragraph, which of the following is closest in meaning to the word "summit"?

*The correct answer is A. In this passage, the word has the same meaning as "top." This question also requires students to use context to determine the meaning of the word.*

5. Based on its usage in the fifth paragraph, which of the following is closest in meaning to the word "resembles"?

*The correct answer is B. In this passage, the word has the same meaning as "looks like." This question also requires students to use context to determine the meaning of the word.*

## Extra practice

To help your child work on the skills assessed by this standard, try this activity:

1. Charles Dickens is considered one of the master storytellers of the English language. However, his works were written about 150 years ago, and many feature words that may not be recognizable by young readers. Select a work by Charles Dickens using your local library or online resource; good choices for young readers include *Great Expectations*, *A Christmas Carol*, and *David Copperfield*.

2. Ask your child to read aloud the first page of the book. Then ask your child to point out any unfamiliar words or phrases. For each word or phrase, prompt your child to use context clues to try to determine the meaning. (Even if your child cannot determine the exact meaning, he or she may be able to figure out that the word is a noun or verb, for example.)

3. Look up the definitions for all unfamiliar words. Ask your child to make a list of all the new words he or she has encountered, along with their definitions.

Through this activity, your child will be directly practicing the skills covered by the standard. He or she will encounter unfamiliar words and attempt to figure out what they mean by using clues in the surrounding text and certain Latin or Greek affixes that might be contained within the words. In addition, your child will expand her vocabulary by and defining new words.

As you read with your child, practice these skills to figure out word meaning. Remind them of these steps:

1. Look for context clues. Begin with the adjacent words and phrases and then move to nearby phrases and sentences.
2. Visualize the word or what is being described to help put the word in context.
3. Look for root words. Are there words that sound or look similar to the unfamiliar word?
4. Consider the various meanings of multiple-meaning words. Does the first meaning that comes to mind make sense in the sentence?
5. Look for other places that an unfamiliar word is used. If it is used more than once in the text, the other places might help confirm its meaning.

Look for opportunities to further explore word meaning with your child. Encourage your child to use the word in a sentence. Or ask a question that helps your child relate the word to what he or she knows (e.g. "Have you heard the word *volunteer* used before? If so, when?").

As children read, they will naturally build their vocabulary. Being able to use a variety of strategies to determine word meaning will help them meet the goals of the standard and be better readers across all disciplines.

## ? Quiz

Have your child read this passage and answer the questions that follow.

## READ *Mexico* by Margaret Duncan Coxhead (excerpt)

In the land of Anahuac settled a roaming people whose story we can only dimly guess. If they came from the wintry north, this country, which is now called Mexico, must have seemed a paradise on earth. Between two high mountain ranges stretches a lofty plateau, beautiful alike in scenery and climate. Lying a bare twenty degrees north of the equator, it would be hot as the plains of India if it were not for its altitude. Such a height, indeed, in the latitude of New York would mean an Arctic climate, but to Mexico it gives almost perpetual spring. Midway across the plateau is a valley with five fair lakes, while from the snow-capped mountains rivers flow eastward to the Atlantic and westward to the Pacific.

Almost all early civilisations have taken their rise in warm, well-watered lands, not too ener-vating in climate. In Egypt, China, Chaldea, the people gained an easy livelihood from the rich al-luvial soil, and had time to think of arts and crafts. So it was in Anahuac, whose very name means near the water. While the Indians of North America endured all the hardships and uncertainties of a hunter's life, the dwellers in this sunnier land learned to till the soil, and then, rewarded by its rich yield, had leisure and strength to invent many an art which added to the beauty and comfort of life. Lost is the history of these primitive inhabitants, but massive ruins of palaces, temples, and pyramids, ancient perhaps as those of Egypt, bear witness to their skill.

Earliest of the settlers in Anahuac, from whom tradition tries to lift the veil, were the Toltecs. From "an ancient red land" they came far away in the north, driven from their home by their fierce neighbours the Chichimecs. They were led by seven chieftains but God was their great commander, and from the stars Hueman, their high priest, read His will. A hundred years they wandered before they reached the land of Anahuac, and founded there, towards the close of the seventh century, a wonderful empire. North of the valley of the five lakes they built their capital Tula. So many and so fine were their palaces and temples that the name Toltec became a synonym for architect. In astrology, soothsaying, and the calculation of time, they were well versed. "The aged Hueman," who must have lived three hundred years, or had successors of the same name, "assembled all the wise men to join him in his final work on earth" some time after the foundation of the empire. Together they prepared the "Book of God," in which they represented by paintings every event in their history from the Creation to their arrival at Tula. In this divine book, which, unfortunately, is known to us only through tradition, they depicted their knowledge of agriculture, of metal-working, and of other arts, their system of government, the rites of their religion, their reading of the stars, and mystical prophecies concerning the future.

The Toltecs were not warlike, and after four hundred years their empire seems to have melted away before the onslaughts of the Chichimecs who had followed them from the north. Savage and ignorant, the new-comers lived only on game and natural roots and fruits, were clothed only in the skins of beasts, and had no weapons save the bow and arrow. Their sway in Anahuac was short, for they were speedily followed and absorbed by more civilized tribes, worthier successors to the Toltecs, who still lingered in the land of their lost empire.

# Questions

1. Based on its usage in the passage, which of the following is closest in meaning to the word "lofty"?

   A. high
   B. low
   C. hill
   D. beautiful

2. Based on its usage in the passage, which of the following is closest in meaning to the word "dwellers"?

   A. farmers
   B. herders
   C. inhabitants
   D. families

3. Based on its usage in the passage, which of the following is closest in meaning to the word "chieftains"?

   A. parents
   B. people
   C. enemies
   D. leaders

4. Based on its usage in the passage, which of the following is closest in meaning to the word "agriculture"?

A. *hunting*

B. *metal-working*

C. *farming*

D. *tradition*

5. In the fourth paragraph, what does it mean when it says that the Toltec empire "melted away"?

A. *The climate got hotter.*

B. *The empire disappeared.*

C. *All the ice was gone.*

D. *There was no more snow.*

# ✓ Answers

1. Based on its usage in the passage, which of the following is closest in meaning to the word "lofty"?

   *The correct answer is A. "High" has the same meaning as "lofty" in this sentence. The "lofty" plateau was between two "high" mountains.*

2. Based on its usage in the passage, which of the following is closest in meaning to the word "dwellers"?

   *The correct answer is C. "Inhabitants" has the same meaning as "dwellers" because the it's referring to the people who lived "in this sunnier land."*

3. Based on its usage in the passage, which of the following is closest in meaning to the word "chieftains"?

   *The correct answer is D. "Leaders" has the same meaning as "chieftains" in this sentence.*

4. Based on its usage in the passage, which of the following is closest in meaning to the word "agriculture"?

   *The correct answer is C. "Farming" has the same meaning as "agriculture." Earlier in the passage, it describes how the Toltecs "learned to till the soil."*

5. In the fourth paragraph, what does it mean when it says that the Toltec empire "melted away"?

   *The correct answer is B. In this paragraph, the phrase "their empire seems to have melted away" means that the empire disappeared, just like an ice cube disappears after it melts. The rest of the fourth paragraph talks about how the Toltec empire may have conquered by its enemies.*

# THE STANDARD

*RL.5.1: Quotes and Inferences – Literature*
*Quote accurately from a text when explaining what the text says explicitly and when drawing inferences from the text.*

## What does it mean?

This literature standard focuses on a child's ability to quote details and examples to illustrate what the text is about.

## Try this together

Here's a brief story about a house that just might hold dark secrets. To address this reading standard, a teacher might ask questions such as the ones that follow the story, or assign them as homework. We have provided possible answers in the "Answers" section, along with an explanation of how the questions connect to the standard.

Before trying this exercise with your child, read through the story and the questions that follow it. Then have your child read the story aloud to you and the answer the questions. Talk about the answers together. Help your child notice how he or she can find answers to questions by looking back at the story.

 **Haunted**

The three boys stood in front of the decaying two-story house. The grass in the front yard was tall and brittle, and the windows were nothing but jagged shards. The wooden stairs leading up to the front porch sagged heavily in the middle, as if they might give way under the slightest weight.

"I'm not going in there," Bradley said.

"You have to," said Jace. "That was the bet. You agreed that if you lost, you would go in there for five minutes alone."

"Yeah," said Bradley, "but I only lost because you cheated."

"How do you cheat at chess?" asked Jace.

The third boy, Marcus, stepped forward onto the sidewalk in front of the house. "I'll go in with you," he said. When Bradley heard Marcus's offer, he sighed with relief.

"That's not fair," Jace said. "He's supposed to do it alone."

"He will," Marcus said. "And so will I. We'll just both do it alone at the same time. Bradley, you go upstairs, and I'll stay downstairs."

Jace thought this over. "Yeah, I guess that's okay. But I'm not starting the timer until Bradley's upstairs."

Marcus hopped onto the porch first, skipping over the sagging steps. The paint on the outside of the house, which had once been white, was gray and flaking away. The front door handle was covered in something slimy and black that made it difficult to turn. Marcus used both hands and finally got the door to open.

Inside, the house was dark and still. The front room was filled with old furniture that had been shredded by mice and raccoons. The faded wallpaper had peeled away from the wall in wide strips, revealing moldy wood and plaster underneath. The smell of the place reminded Marcus of his brother's dirty socks.

Marcus turned toward the front door to call out to Bradley. "Come on in!" he said. Through the open door he could see Bradley nervously making his way up the porch. But just as Bradley reached the front doorway, a blast of cold wind shot through the house and slammed the front door shut.

With the door closed, the house got darker. Marcus felt along the wall to find his way back out. Suddenly, he heard something upstairs.

It was the sound of footsteps.

# ❓ Questions

1. What phrase does the author use to describe the grass in front of the abandoned house?

   _____

   _____

2. What line of dialogue reveals that two of the boys played chess?

   _____

   _____

3. Which sentence describes what was wrong with the door handle?

   _____

   _____

4. Which sentence reveals that the house has an unpleasant smell?

   _____

   _____

5. What inference can be made at the end of the story?

   _____

   _____

   _____

   _____

# ✓ Answers

1. What phrase does the author use to describe the grass in front of the abandoned house?

   *The correct answer is "tall and brittle." This question requires students to quote accurately from the text when explaining what the text says, as dictated by the standard.*

2. What line of dialogue reveals that two of the boys played chess?

   *The correct answer is "How do you cheat at chess?" This question requires students to quote accurately from the text but also requires them to draw inferences, or make an educated guess.*

3. Which sentence describes what was wrong with the door handle?

   *The correct answer is "The front door handle was covered in something slimy and black that made it difficult to turn." This question also requires students to quote accurately from the text when explaining what the text says.*

4. Which sentence reveals that the house has an unpleasant smell?

   *The correct answer is "The smell of the place reminded Marcus of his brother's dirty socks." This question also requires students to quote accurately from the text when explaining what the text says, as dictated by the standard.*

5. What inference can be made at the end of the story?

   *Answers will vary but should include the idea that someone else is in the house other than the three boys. This question requires students to draw inferences, or make an educated guess, based on details in the story.*

## Extra practice

To help your child work on the skills assessed by this standard, try this activity:

1. Ask your child to choose a favorite book or story.
2. Then ask your child to open the book or story to a random page, and select some interesting details from the text.
3. Next, ask your child to imagine that he or she is interviewing a character in the book or story. Ask your child to write interview questions that can be answered by quoting the details from the story. For example, using the story from this lesson, a reporter might ask Marcus, "What did the front room of the abandoned house look like?" His answer would be, "The front room was filled with old furniture that had been shredded by mice and raccoons. The faded wallpaper had peeled away from the wall in wide strips, revealing moldy wood and plaster underneath."

Through this activity, your child will be directly practicing the skills covered by the standard. He or she will see how details can be used to support ideas in a story.

## ? Quiz

Have your child read this passage and write the answers independently in the space provided.

 *Treasure Island* **by Robert Louis Stevenson (excerpt)**

Perhaps it was this—perhaps it was the look of the island, with its grey, melancholy woods, and wild stone spires, and the surf that we could both see and hear foaming and thundering on the steep beach—at least, although the sun shone bright and hot, and the shore birds were fishing and crying all around us, and you would have thought anyone would have been glad to get to land after being so long at sea, my heart sank, as the saying is, into my boots; and from the first look onward, I hated the very thought of Treasure Island.

We had a dreary morning's work before us, for there was no sign of any wind, and the boats had to be got out and manned, and the ship warped three or four miles round the corner of the island and up the narrow passage to the haven behind Skeleton Island. I volunteered for one of the boats, where I had, of course, no business. The heat was sweltering, and the men grumbled fiercely over their work. Anderson was in command of my boat, and instead of keeping the crew in order, he grumbled as loud as the worst.

"Well," he said with an oath, "it's not forever."

I thought this was a very bad sign, for up to that day the men had gone briskly and willingly about their business; but the very sight of the island had relaxed the cords of discipline.

All the way in, Long John stood by the steersman and conned the ship. He knew the passage like the palm of his hand, and though the man in the chains got everywhere more water than was down in the chart, John never hesitated once.

"There's a strong scour with the ebb," he said, "and this here passage has been dug out, in a manner of speaking, with a spade."

We brought up just where the anchor was in the chart, about a third of a mile from each shore, the mainland on one side and Skeleton Island on the other. The bottom was clean sand. The plunge of our anchor sent up clouds of birds wheeling and crying over the woods, but in less than a minute they were down again and all was once more silent.

## ? Questions

1. How does the speaker describe his feelings toward the island?
   A. "the sun shone bright and hot"
   B. "shore birds were fishing and crying all around us"
   C. "I hated the very thought of Treasure Island"
   D. "grey, melancholy"

2. What phrase reveals that the boats had to be rowed to shore?
   A. "for there was no sign of any wind, and the boats had to be got out and manned"
   B. "I volunteered for one of the boats"
   C. "Anderson was in command of my boat"
   D. "Long John stood by the steersman and conned the ship"

3. How did the behavior of the crew men change from the day before?
   A. The day before they were happy, but today they are upset.
   B. The day before they didn't want to go to Treasure Island, but today they are excited to be there.
   C. The day before they were mad at Anderson, but today they have forgiven him.
   D. The day before they worked hard, but today they are undisciplined.

4. What phrase reveals that Long John knew Treasure Island well?
   A. "Long John stood by the steersman and conned the ship"
   B. "the ship warped three or four miles round the corner of the island and up the narrow passage"
   C. "He knew the passage like the palm of his hand"
   D. "the man in the chains got everywhere more water than was down in the chart"

5. Where was the anchor in the chart?
   A. "about a third of a mile from each shore, the mainland on one side and Skeleton Island on the other"
   B. "over the woods"
   C. "three or four miles round the corner of the island"
   D. "up the narrow passage to the haven behind Skeleton Island"

# ✓ Answers

1. How does the speaker describe his feelings toward the island?
   *The correct answer is C. At the end of the first paragraph, the speaker says that he "hated the very thought of Treasure Island." This response requires an accurate quote from the passage.*

2. What phrase reveals that the boats had to be rowed to shore?
   *The correct answer is A. The beginning of the second paragraph mentions that there wasn't any wind and the boat still had to travel "three or four miles," so they had to row the boats. This response requires an accurate quote from the passage.*

3. How did the behavior of the crew men change from the day before?
   *The correct answer is D. In the fourth paragraph, the speaker says, "up to that day the men had gone briskly and willingly about their business; but the very sight of the island had relaxed the cords of discipline." This response requires an accurate quote from the passage.*

4. What phrase reveals that Long John knew Treasure Island well?

   *The correct answer is C. Your child should use context clues to understand that saying someone knows something "like the palm of his hand" means that he's very familiar with it. This response requires an accurate quote from the passage.*

5. Where was the anchor in the chart?

   *The correct answer is A. The final paragraph of the passage says this directly. This response requires an accurate quote from the passage.*

# THE STANDARD

*RL.5.2: Theme – Literature*
*Determine a theme of a story, drama, or poem from details in the text, including how characters in a story or drama respond to challenges or how the speaker in a poem reflects upon a topic; summarize the text.*

## What does it mean?

This literature standard focuses on a child's ability to identify the theme of a passage and to provide a summary of it.

## Try this together

Here's a brief story that focuses on a specific theme. To address this reading standard, a teacher might ask questions such as the ones that follow the story, or assign them as homework. We have provided possible answers in the "Answers" section, along with an explanation of how the questions connect to the standard.

Before trying this exercise with your child, read through the story and the questions that follow it. Then have your child read the story aloud to you and the answer the questions. Talk about the answers together. Help your child notice how she can find answers to questions by looking back at the story.

 **One Little Lie**

Tori was so excited to go on the field trip to the zoo. She couldn't wait to see the elephants, lions, and giraffes. However, when she got to school on the morning of the trip, she realized that she had forgotten to ask her mother to sign the permission slip. Without a signed permission slip, she would not be allowed to go. The buses were already waiting in the parking lot and her mother was already at work, so she couldn't go back home to get it signed.

"What are you going to do?" asked her best friend Jill.

Tori grabbed a pen and signed her mother's name to the permission slip.

"You can't do that!" Jill said.

"It's just one little lie," Tori said. "My mom would totally let me go. I just forgot to ask her."

When Tori handed the permission slip to Mr. Dunphy, he eyed it suspiciously. "Tori, this doesn't look like your mother's signature," he said.

Tori had to think fast. "Oh," she said, "that's because she had to sign it with her other hand.

She . . . broke her arm." Tori hated making up a lie like that, but she had to come up with a reason to explain the false signature.

Mr. Dunphy was very concerned. "Oh my," he said. "What happened?"

"It was a . . . a car accident," Tori said.

"Is she okay?" he asked. "She's supposed to volunteer at the bake sale tomorrow. I should call her and check on her."

"Don't do that!" said Tori, panicked. Now she had to think of another lie to keep Mr. Dunphy from calling her mom and uncovering her deception. "Her phone got broken. In the accident."

Mr. Dunphy narrowed his eyes. Was he catching on? "Luckily," he said, "we have the phone number of the office where she works." He left the classroom and went up to the principal's office.

"Uh oh," Jill said.

Tori was terrified. She had no idea what was going to happen next. How many lies would she have to tell to get out of this? Was there any way out?

When Mr. Dunphy came back, his face was stern. "Tori, I just spoke to your mother," he said. "Do you have anything you'd like to tell me?"

Tori stared at the ground. "I'm sorry," she said. "I forgot to have my mom sign the slip, and I wanted to go on the trip so badly. And then I had to tell more lies to cover up the first one."

Mr. Dunphy nodded. "Thank you for finally being honest. If you'd just told the truth in the first place, we wouldn't have had a problem. See?" He held up a slip of paper. "I had your mother fax a copy of the permission slip from her office to the principal's office."

Tori gasped. "I can still go on the trip?"

Mr. Dunphy smiled. "Yes, you can go. But promise me you'll remember this the next time you think about lying."

# ❓ Questions

1. What is the theme of this story?

   _____

   _____

   _____

   _____

2. In three sentences or less, summarize the events that occur in the story.

   _____

   _____

   _____

   _____

3. How does Tori respond to the problems she encounters?

   _____

   _____

   _____

   _____

4.  How does Jill respond to Tori's behavior?

_____

_____

_____

_____

5.  How does Mr. Dunphy's solution to Tori's problem emphasize the theme?

_____

_____

_____

_____

 **Answers**

1.  What is the theme of this story?

    _Answers will vary but should include the idea of honesty being the best course of action, or that lies can result in ever-growing problems. This question requires students to identify the theme or lesson about life, conveyed through story events._

2.  In three sentences or less, summarize the events that occur in the passage.

    _Answers will vary but should include some elements found in the following sample: Tori discovers that she forgot to have her mom sign her permission slip for a field trip. She forges her mom's signature, which leads to her having to come up with other lies. In the end, she realizes that she should have been honest with her teacher from the beginning. This question requires students to summarize the passage. Note that this is different from expressing the theme; although the details of the passage reinforce the theme, a summary of the passage focuses on important events that happen._

3.  How does Tori respond to the problems she encounters?

    _Tori responds to her problems by lying. This changes at the very end, where she faces her problems and finally tells her teacher the truth. This question requires students to draw on details from the story explain how a character responds to a challenge._

4.  How does Jill respond to Tori's behavior?

    _Jill tries to keep Tori from lying. This is another question that requires students to draw on details to explain how a character responds to a challenge._

5.  How does Mr. Dunphy's solution to Tori's problem emphasize the theme?

    _If Tori had told the truth from the beginning, Mr. Dunphy could have obtained a signed permission slip from Tori's mom without all the problems that Tori brought on herself. This question requires students to draw a connection between a specific detail and the theme._

# Extra practice

To help your child work on the skills assessed by this standard, try this activity:

1. Ask your child to think of a theme, such as "Nature can help a person forget their worries" or "Love between family members is unconditional." Then ask your child to create a list of words, examples, and situations that might reflect this theme.

2. Next, ask your child to write a short poem based on the theme. (It doesn't have to rhyme!) Here's the most important part: The poem CANNOT state what the theme is; instead, it should suggest or emphasize the theme through description, events, and so on.

3. Ask your child to read the poem aloud to a friend and see if the friend can figure out the theme.

Through this activity your child will be directly practicing the skills covered by the standard. He or she will recognize how a theme is suggested by details within a literary work\ and will be able to better understand the techniques used by authors when conveying a theme.

## Quiz

Have your child read this passage and write the answers independently in the space provided.

 ***The Adventures of Danny Meadow Mouse* by Thornton W. Burgess (excerpt)**

All Danny Meadow Mouse could think about was his short tail. He was so ashamed of it that whenever any one passed, he crawled out of sight so that they should not see how short his tail is. Instead of playing in the sunshine as he used to do, he sat and sulked. Pretty soon his friends began to pass without stopping. Finally one day old Mr. Toad sat down in front of Danny and began to ask questions.

"What's the matter?" asked old Mr. Toad.

"Nothing," replied Danny Meadow Mouse.

"I don't suppose that there really is anything the matter, but what do you think is the matter?" said old Mr. Toad.

Danny fidgeted, and old Mr. Toad looked up at jolly, round, red Mr. Sun and winked. "Sun is just as bright as ever, isn't it?" he inquired.

"Yes," said Danny.

"Got plenty to eat and drink, haven't you?" continued Mr. Toad.

"Yes," said Danny.

"Seems to me that that is a pretty good looking suit of clothes you're wearing," said Mr. Toad, eyeing Danny critically. "Sunny weather, plenty to eat and drink, and good clothes—must be you don't know when you're well off, Danny Meadow Mouse."

Danny hung his head. Finally he looked up and caught a kindly twinkle in old Mr. Toad's eyes. "Mr. Toad, how can I get a long tail like my cousin Whitefoot of the Green Forest?" he asked.

"So that's what's the matter! Ha! Ha! Ha! Danny Meadow Mouse, I'm ashamed of you! I certainly am ashamed of you!" said Mr. Toad. "What good would a long tail do you? Tell me that."

For a minute Danny didn't know just what to say. "I—I—I'd look so much better if I had a long tail," he ventured.

Old Mr. Toad just laughed. "You never saw a Meadow Mouse with a long tail, did you? Of course not. What a sight it would be! Why, everybody on the Green Meadows would laugh themselves sick at the sight! You see you need to be slim and trim and handsome to carry a long tail well. And then what a nuisance it would be! You would always have to be thinking of your tail and taking care to keep it out of harm's way. Look at me. I'm homely. Some folks call me ugly to look at. But no one tries to catch me as Farmer Brown's boy does Billy Mink because of his fine coat; and no one wants to put me in a cage because of a fine voice. I am satisfied to be just as I am, and if you'll take my advice, Danny Meadow Mouse, you'll be satisfied to be just as you are."

"Perhaps you are right," said Danny Meadow Mouse after a little. "I'll try."

# ❓ Questions

1. What is the theme of this passage?

    A. *Someone else is always better off than you.*

    B. *Practice makes perfect.*

    C. *Be happy with yourself and what you have.*

    D. *Toads give the best advice.*

2. What is the best summary of this passage?

    A. *Danny's tail is broken, and Mr. Toad helps him heal it.*

    B. *Mr. Toad is feeling self-conscious because people call him ugly, and Danny helps him feel better about himself.*

    C. *Danny and his cousin get into a fight, and Mr. Toad helps settle the argument.*

    D. *Danny is feeling self-conscious because his tail is short, and Mr. Toad helps him realize that his tail is perfect the way it is.*

3. Why does Mr. Toad talk about the sun and Danny's clothes?

    A. *He thinks Danny is dressed inappropriately for the weather.*

    B. *He is helping Danny realize that he has many good things to be thankful for.*

    C. *It is raining, and Danny's clothes are wet.*

    D. *Mr. Toad envies how Danny's clothes look in the sun.*

4. How is the theme reinforced by Mr. Toad saying that he is "ashamed" of Danny?
   A. *Danny is being envious of his cousin and not appreciating why his tail is better short.*
   B. *Mr. Toad wishes he had a tail and thinks Danny shouldn't complain.*
   C. *Mr. Toad is tired of Danny complaining about things.*
   D. *Mr. Toad things Danny's short tail is ugly.*

5. The theme of this story applies to which characters?
   A. *only Danny*
   B. *only Mr. Toad*
   C. *Both Danny and Mr. Toad*
   D. *Neither Danny nor Mr. Toad*

## ✓ Answers

1. What is the theme of this passage?

   *The correct answer is C. This sentence states the theme of the passage. Danny wants a long tail like his cousin, and Mr. Toad helps him realize that Danny has much to be happy about just the way he is.*

2. What is the best summary of this passage?

   *The correct answer is D. This is the best summary of what happened in the passage. Your child might notice that other choices match details from the passage, but they don't summarize it.*

3. Why does Mr. Toad talk about the sun and Danny's clothes?

   *The correct answer is B. By mentioning that the sun is shining and that Danny is wearing nice clothes, Mr. Toad is helping Danny realize that he has much to be thankful for and that he should not be envious of his cousin.*

4. How is the theme reinforced by Mr. Toad saying that he is "ashamed" of Danny?

   *The correct answer is A. Mr. Toad is telling Danny that he shouldn't envy his cousin's long tail. Meadow mice don't have long tails.*

5. The theme of this story applies to which characters?

   *The correct answer is C. The theme of this story applies to both characters. Mr. Toad is glad to be considered "homely" because it means he isn't hunted by the farmers. Danny should be glad that his tail is short because meadow mice are better suited to having short tails.*

# THE STANDARD

**RL.5.3:** *Compare and Contrast Characters and Story Elements – Literature*
*Compare and contrast two or more characters, settings, or events in a story or drama, drawing on specific details in the text (e.g., how characters interact).*

## What does it mean?

This literature standard focuses on a child's ability to compare characters, settings, and events using details to help explain similarities and differences.

## Try this together

Here's a brief story that focuses on two different characters. To address this reading standard, a teacher might ask questions such as the ones that follow the story, or assign them as homework. We have provided possible answers in the "Answers" section, along with an explanation of how the questions connect to the standard.

Before trying this exercise with your child, read through the story and the questions that follow it. Then have your child read the story aloud to you and the answer the questions. Talk about the answers together. Help your child notice how he or she can find answers to questions by looking back at the story.

 **Twinnies**

Maria and Monica were identical twins, and they were starting to hate it. All throughout their childhood, they always had to wear the same outfits and play with the same friends. Worst of all, everyone always got them mixed up—even relatives! Before they started sixth grade, they both decided to make sure no one would confuse them again. Maria decided to dress in sweatshirts and jeans all the time. Monica chose to wear button-down shirts and long skirts instead. Maria kept her hair back in a ponytail, while Monica let hers hang down over her shoulders.

They also tried to arrange their class schedules so that they were on opposite sides of the school throughout the day. They hardly even saw each other at school. This allowed their classmates to get to know them as individuals. Maria signed up for soccer and glee club; Monica joined the cheerleading squad and the school newspaper staff. Maria made lots of friends that did not even know she had a twin sister, and so did Monica.

A few weeks after school started, Maria heard that the school was forming a math team to compete in events with other local schools. Maria always loved math, so she decided that she would sign up. Her new friends, however, were skeptical.

"Why would you do math when you're not even being graded on it?" her new friend Shelly asked.

But Maria was determined to join the math team, so she went to the first meeting of the math club after school. When she sat down, she was surprised to see her twin sister Monica there as well. "What are you doing here?" Maria asked.

"I've always loved math," Monica said. "You know that. I tried to convince some of my new friends to come, but they weren't interested. To them, math is a chore."

"Really?" Maria asked. She realized that no matter what, she and her sister were very much alike. And that was okay, after all. She smiled at her sister. "We said we were going to stay apart at school this year," she said. "But maybe, in this case, we can share."

# Questions

1.  Compare and contrast Maria's and Monica's appearance.

   _____

   _____

   _____

   _____

2.  How do Maria and Monica's choices of after-school activities reflect their different interests?

   _____

   _____

   _____

   _____

3.  How does the fact that both girls show up to join the math team reflect their personalities?

   _____

   _____

   _____

   _____

4.  What do Maria's and Monica's new friends have in common?

   _____

   _____

   _____

   _____

5. What do the girls' different clothing choices reveal about their personalities?

_____

_____

_____

_____

## ✓ Answers

*1.* Compare and contrast Maria's and Monica's appearance.

*Maria wears casual clothes such as sweatshirts and jeans, and keeps her hair in a pony-tail. Monica wears more formal clothing and leaves her hair down. This question requires students to draw on details in the passage that describe the differences between the two characters, just as the standard dictates.*

*2.* How do Maria and Monica's choices of after-school activities reflect their different interests?

*Maria is interested in sports and music, while Monica is interested in writing and cheerleading. This question requires students to use details to help contrast the two characters.*

*3.* How does the fact that both girls show up to join the math team reflect their personalities?

*Despite their differences, both girls are still very much alike in some ways. This question requires students to draw an inference based on details from the story.*

*4.* What do Maria's and Monica's new friends have in common?

*Both girls end up with friends that have no interest in math. This question also requires students to draw an inference based on details; this allows students to realize the strong similarity between the two groups of friends.*

*5.* What do the girls' different clothing choices reveal about their personalities?

*Answers will vary, but should show reasoning that supports the student's answer. Maria's clothing choices suggest that she is more easygoing and less conscious of her appearance, while Monica seems to be very concerned about always looking her best. This question is more complex than the previous questions. It requires students to take details from the text and use those details to infer major character traits of the two main characters.*

# Extra practice

To help your child work on the skills assessed by this standard, try this activity:

1. Ask your child to think about his or her last two birthdays.
2. Then ask your child to make a list of all the ways in which the two events were similar.
3. Finally, ask your child to make another list of all the ways in which the two events were different from each other.

Through this activity your child will be directly practicing the skills covered by the standard. He or she will learn to compare and contrast events and will be better equipped to understand how authors use these same techniques when describing events in stories.

## Quiz

Have your child read this passage and write the answers independently in the space provided.

### *The Husband of the Rat's Daughter* by Leonora Alleyne (Mrs. Andrew Lang) (excerpt)

Once upon a time there lived in Japan a rat and his wife who came of an old and noble race, and had one daughter, the loveliest girl in all the rat world. Her parents were very proud of her, and spared no pains to teach her all she ought to know. There was not another young lady in the whole town who was as clever as she was in gnawing through the hardest wood, or who could drop from such a height on to a bed, or run away so fast if anyone was heard coming. Great attention, too, was paid to her personal appearance, and her skin shone like satin, while her teeth were as white as pearls, and beautifully pointed.

Of course, with all these advantages, her parents expected her to make a brilliant marriage, and as she grew up, they began to look round for a suitable husband.

But here a difficulty arose. The father was a rat from the tip of his nose to the end of his tail, outside as well as in, and desired that his daughter should wed among her own people. She had no lack of lovers, but her father's secret hopes rested on a fine young rat, with moustaches which almost swept the ground, which family was still more nobler and ancient than his own. Unluckily, the mother had other views for her precious child. She was one of those people who always despise their own family and surroundings, and take pleasure in thinking that they themselves are made of finer material than the rest of the world. "Her daughter should never marry a mere rat," she declared, holding her head high. "With her beauty and talents she had a right to look for someone a little better than that."

So she talked, as mothers will, to anyone that would listen to her. What the girl thought about the matter nobody knew or cared —it was not the fashion in the rat world. Many were the quarrels which the old rat and his wife had upon the subject[. . .]

"Reach up to the stars is my motto," cried the lady one day, when she was in a greater passion than usual. "My daughter's beauty places her higher than anything upon earth," she cried; "and I am certainly not going to accept a son-in-law who is beneath her."

"Better offer her in marriage to the sun," answered her husband impatiently. "As far as I know there is nothing greater than him."

"Well, I was thinking of it," replied the wife, "and as you are of the same mind, we will pay him a visit tomorrow."

# Questions

1. What are the mother rat and the father rat's thoughts about their daughter's potential husband?
   A. *The father rat wants his daughter to marry the sun, and the mother rat disapproves.*
   B. *The mother rat wants her daughter to marry someone with a good personality, and the father rat wants his daughter to marry someone from a good family.*
   C. *The mother rat and father rat both want their daughter to marry the sun.*
   D. *The father rat wants his daughter to marry another rat, and the mother rat wants her daughter to marry someone who is not a rat.*

2. What do the mother rat and the father rat have in common?
   A. *They both want their daughter to marry someone she loves.*
   B. *They want their daughter to become more beautiful.*
   C. *They are both proud of their daughter.*
   D. *The both want their daughter to marry the sun.*

3. How does each rat parent feel about the sun marrying their daughter?
   A. *The mother rat says it as a joke, and the father rat thinks it could really happen.*
   B. *The father rat says it as a joke, and the mother rat thinks it could really happen.*
   C. *Both rat parents are excited about it.*
   D. *The mother rat was persuaded by the father rat to try it.*

4. Why does the mother rat think her daughter should not marry another rat?
   A. *No other rat family is nobler than their own.*
   B. *No rat would marry her.*
   C. *She is more beautiful and talented than the other rats.*
   D. *Her father wouldn't like it.*

5. With which parent does the daughter rat agree?
   A. *Her mother*
   B. *Her father*
   C. *Both parents*
   D. *It is unknown*

# ✔ Answers

1. What are the mother rat and the father rat's thoughts about their daughter's potential husband?

   *The correct answer is D. The mother rat says that her daughter "should never marry a mere rat," while the father rat's "secret hopes rested on a fine young rat" from a good family.*

2. What do the mother rat and the father rat have in common?

   *The correct answer is C. The first paragraph says this directly ("Her parents were very proud of her").*

3. How does each rat parent feel about the sun marrying their daughter?

   *The correct answer is B. The father rat mentions marrying their daughter to the sun as a joke because "there is nothing greater than him [the sun]." The mother rat thinks the father rat is being serious and decides that it would be a good idea.*

4. Why does the mother rat think her daughter should not marry another rat?

   *The correct answer is C. In the third paragraph, the mother rat mentions her daughter's "beauty and talents." She believes that these are great qualities and that her daughter shouldn't have to marry a "mere rat."*

5. With which parent does the daughter rat agree?

   *The correct answer is D. The passage does not say what the daughter thinks about whom she should marry. In the fourth paragraph, the narrator says that "nobody knew or cared" what the daughter thought.*

# THE STANDARD

**RL.5.4:** *Vocabulary – Literature*
*Determine the meaning of words and phrases as they are used in a text, including figurative language such as metaphors and similes.*

## What does it mean?

This literature standard focuses on a child's ability to determine the meanings of words and phrases as they are used in a passage. This includes an examination of words and phrases that have either a literal or figurative meaning. Two types of figurative languages are metaphors ("the stars are diamonds in the sky") and similes ("she swims like a fish").

## Try this together

Here's a brief story about an encounter with a mysterious old woman. To address this reading standard, a teacher might ask questions such as the ones that follow the passage, or assign them as homework. We have provided possible answers in the "Answers" section, along with an explanation of how the questions connect to the standard.

Before trying this exercise with your child, read through the story and the questions that follow it. Then have your child read the story aloud to you and the answer the questions. Talk about the answers together. Help your child notice how he or she can find answers to questions by looking back at the story.

## The Witch of Newcombe

It was raining cats and dogs the night I first met the Witch of Newcombe. I was on my way home from work when the dark skies opened up without warning, unleashing sheets of rain all at once. I ducked under the covered porch of a tall old house a few steps off the sidewalk, hoping to wait out the rain.

Right away, the porch light flashed on. The front door opened just a crack, and a single blue eye stared out at me. It was surrounded by wrinkles. "Are you making mischief out there?" the old woman behind the door asked.

"No," I said. "I was just trying to get out of the rain."

The blue eye looked me over, squinted and disappeared as the door shut. Then the door swung wide. "Come in then," she said. "No sense leaving you out in this mess."

She was short and hunched over, and walked with the help of a cane made from a tree branch. She had long hair as white as bone, braided into a thick rope that hung down her back.

"Thank you for inviting me inside," I said. "That was very kind."

She waved off the compliment as if it were a fly buzzing around her head. "Despite what some people in this neighborhood might say, I do not have a heart of stone.

I help people get the thing they crave most in the world."

"What is that?" I asked.

"It's different for every person," she said. "Sometimes, it's money. Often, it's love. Some people crave fame. Others crave respect."

"How do you help people get the thing they crave most?"

"It's simple," she said, and smiled. "I just use magic."

# ❓ Questions

1. Based on its usage in the story, which of the following is closest in meaning to the word "mischief"?

   A. measurements

   B. good deeds

   C. trouble

   D. joke

2. Based on its usage in the story, which of the following is closest in meaning to the word "crave"?

   A. dislike

   B. desire

   C. award

   D. build

3. In the first paragraph, what does the narrator mean by stating that it was "raining cats and dogs"?

   _____

   _____

   _____

   _____

4. What two things does the narrator compare the old woman's hair to?

   _____

   _____

   _____

   _____

5. When the woman states that she does not have "a heart of stone," what does she mean?

_____

_____

_____

_____

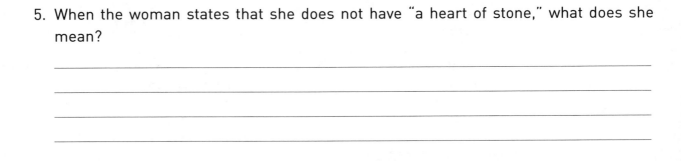 **Answers**

*1.* Based on its usage in the story, which of the following is closest in meaning to the word "mischief"?

*The correct answer is C. In this passage,* mischief *has the same meaning as "trouble." This question requires students to use context clues to determine the literal meaning of a word.*

*2.* Based on its usage in the story, which of the following is closest in meaning to the word "crave"?

*The correct answer is B. In this passage,* crave *has the same meaning as "desire." This question requires students to use context clues to determine the literal meaning of a word*

3. In the first paragraph, what does the narrator mean by stating that it was "raining cats and dogs"?

*A correct response should include the idea that the rainfall was very heavy. This question requires students to understand and explain the meaning behind figurative language. In this case, the figurative language is a popular idiom*

4. What two things does the narrator compare the old woman's hair to?

*A correct response should note that the old woman's hair is compared to bone ("as white as bone") and to a rope ("braided into a thick rope"). This question requires students to understand and explain the meaning behind figurative language. In this case, the figurative language consists of both a simile ("as white as bone") and a metaphor ("braided into a thick rope").*

5. When the woman states that she does not have "a heart of stone," what does she mean?

*A correct response should include the idea that someone with a heart of stone would be considered mean, cruel, or without feeling. For this question, students must understand and explain the figurative meaning of a metaphor ("heart of stone").*

# Extra practice

To help your child work on the skills assessed by this standard, try this activity:

1. Using the Internet or another online resource, help your child look up the lyrics to several popular songs he or she likes.

2. With your child, look through the lyrics for uses of figurative language, particularly metaphors and similes. Make a list of those you find.

3. Ask your child to write down a definition for each word or phrase. If he or she does not know the meaning, give assistance by offering clues from surrounding lyrics or other hints.

Through this activity, your child will be directly practicing the skills covered by the standard. This will help your child deal with words and phrases that mean something beyond their literal definition and will also help expand your child's vocabulary.

## Quiz

Have your child read this passage and write the answers independently in the space provided.

## *The Rowena O'Toole Company* by Ellis Parker Butler (excerpt)

When I was a boy, I had kept rabbits, and they burrowed in Mr. Morton's yard and ate his lettuce crop, which annoying Mr. Morton; and I had had chickens, and they flew over the fence into Mr. Grady's yard and pecked holes in his reddest tomatoes, which displeased Mr. Grady; and so, after I had paid a boy two dollars for a goat, and then paid him fifty cents to take it back because it had eaten to desolation the gardens of both Mr. Morton and Mr. Grady, I consulted those gentlemen as to what manner of animal I had best own next.

The two gentlemen came into my father's back yard by the over-the-fence route. Mr. Grady took a seat on the sawbuck. Mr. Morton leaned against the barn door. Mr. Morton was younger than Mr. Grady, but far more serious. He was studying law, and wore his hair in a broad bang that hung over one eye; and so long I knew him he never smiled. Mr. Grady, on the other hand, was old enough to be young again. He seemed to have no special profession except that of veteran of two fields—Gettysburg and cornfield. He was an ex-soldier and a retired farmer, and as happy by nature as any man could possibly be. I think he lived in cycles of jokes. He would smile all day yesterday thinking the joke he meant to tell some one; to-day he would tell the joke and smile; and to-morrow he would smile over the manner in which the joke was received. The next day he would begin the cycle again. In this way he kept himself always happen and economized his jokes.

"William," said Mr. Morton, when I had stated my indecision, "this matter is one that deserves more than usual consideration, and I must ask you to retire a few moments while Mr. Grady, my honored friend here, and I consult in private."

I knew that meant I was not wanted, and I went into the house – not especially because it was necessary to retire so far, but because there were fresh doughnuts there. When I returned their consultation was completed.

# Questions

1. Based on its usage in the passage, which of the following is closest in meaning to the word "manner"?
   A. politeness
   B. chicken
   C. type
   D. pet

2. Based on its usage in the passage, which of the following is closest in meaning to the word "profession"?
   A. teacher
   B. job
   C. procedure
   D. task

3. Based on its usage in the passage, which of the following is closest in meaning to the word "consult"?
   A. talk
   B. argue
   C. sleep
   D. eat

4. In the first paragraph, what does the narrator mean when he states that the garden was "eaten to desolation"?
   A. he was sad that the garden was eaten
   B. everything in the garden was eaten
   C. everything in the garden died
   D. the farmer cried when the garden was eaten

5. In the third paragraph, what does it mean when the narrator is asked to "retire a few moments"?
   A. The two men want the narrator to take a short nap.
   B. The narrator should stop working.
   C. The two men want the narrator's permission to leave and go to bed.
   D. The two men want the narrator to leave the backyard while they talk.

#  Answers

1. Based on its usage in the passage, which of the following is closest in meaning to the word "manner"?

   *The correct answer is C. "Type" has the same meaning as "manner" in this sentence.*

2. Based on its usage in the passage, which of the following is closest in meaning to the word "profession"?

   *The correct answer is B. "Job" has the same meaning as "profession."*

3. Based on its usage in the passage, which of the following is closest in meaning to the word "consult"?

   *The correct answer is A. "Talk" has the same meaning as "consult."*

4. In the first paragraph, what does the narrator mean when he states that the garden was "eaten to desolation"?

   *The correct answer is B. By saying that the garden was "eaten to desolation," the narrator is describing how his goat ate absolutely everything in the garden. There was nothing left.*

5. In the third paragraph, what does it mean when the narrator is asked to "retire a few moments"?

   *The correct answer is D. In this paragraph, the phrase "retire a few moments" means to leave the backyard. The two men want to talk alone.*

# THE STANDARD

**W.5.1:** *Writing Arguments*
*Write opinion pieces on topics or texts, supporting a point of view with reasons and information.*
**W.5.1.a:** *Introduce a topic or text clearly, state an opinion, and create an organizational structure in which ideas are logically grouped to support the writer's purpose.*
**W.5.1.b:** *Provide logically ordered reasons that are supported by facts and details.*
**W.5.1.c:** *Link opinion and reasons using words, phrases, and clauses (e.g., consequently, specifically).*
**W.5.1.d:** *Provide a concluding statement or section related to the opinion presented.*

## What does it mean?

This standard focuses on a child's ability to write a well-organized paragraph or series of paragraphs. It is designed to assess how well a child can develop a topic by providing appropriate supporting information and make connections between and among the ideas.

The focus of this writing standard is writing an opinion, or argument. Opinion pieces are defined as those in which the writer develops a logical, well-supported argument or claim based on evidence. Sometimes referred to as persuasive writing, these pieces attempt to convince the reader that the ideas and opinions presented are worth adopting.

As shown in the sub-steps of the W.5.1 writing standard, the writing assesses the basic elements of a paragraph or essay, including the introduction (W.5.1a), body (W.5.1.b), and conclusion (W.5.1.d). It also focuses on using words, phrases, and clauses to connect ideas (W.5.1.c).

## Try this together

Regardless of their skill level, all writers get better with practice. Unfortunately, many young writers become overwhelmed when writing is taught all at once. It may help to break down the writing process and focus on one part of the W.5.1 standard at a time. We will look at how this might be done.

Here's a writing prompt similar to one that might be used to test this standard. We have provided a sample answer, along with an explanation of how it all connects to the standard.

# Prompt

*For thousands of years, inventions have made life easier and more rewarding for people. They have also saved countless lives. In your opinion, what is the most important invention ever created, and why? Be sure to include facts and details to support your choice.*

After reading the prompt, have your child to write a topic sentence that states the opinion he or she wants to present.

Next, ask your child to think of facts and details that will help convince readers that the invention chosen is the most important invention ever created. As your child writes these facts and details into the body of the paragraph, encourage him or her to use words and phrases that connect ideas.

Finally, have your child write a concluding sentence. Explain that the conclusion should sum up the main opinion presented in the paragraph. It should not introduce new ideas.

# Sample Answer

*I think the most important invention ever made is the wheel. Wheels allow people to move things from one place to another more easily. Wheels also allow people to travel more freely, which is important in places where food and water are not nearby. Wheels also made it possible to create many kinds of machines, such as pottery wheels. Consequently, pottery wheels allowed people to create vessels for storing water or other things. The basic wheel shape is an important part of gears as well. Plus, if there weren't wheels, I wouldn't be able to skateboard! Without a doubt, the wheel is the most important invention ever made.*

# What's the point?

The main goal of this standard is to encourage students to formulate opinions and back them up with facts and details. Note how in the sample answer, the student provides several distinct reasons why wheels are the most important invention ever made. These reasons can be subjective; for example, most people would not list skateboards as one of the main reasons why wheels are the most important invention. However, it is important to provide reasons with as much specific detail as possible. Simply stating "Wheels are important because they are everywhere" would not be sufficient for this standard.

Also note that words and phrases, such as *consequently, specifically,* and *plus,* help link the ideas together, and that the concluding sentence restates the main opinion presented in the paragraph.

# Extra practice

To help your child work on the skills assessed by this standard, try this activity:

1. Ask your child to pick a topic about which he or she has a strong opinion. It can be as simple as whether or not teachers should give out homework, or as complex as the issue of freedom of speech on the Internet. Ask him or her to write down a list of reasons and facts that support that viewpoint.

2. Next, ask your child to take a new sheet of paper and place it next to the original list. Now, ask your child to put him- or herself in the position of someone who feels the exact opposite of the way she does. If your child thinks teachers should not be allowed to assign after-school work, your child should try to imagine someone who thinks after-school work should be required. Ask your son or daughter to make a list of the most compelling reasons to support that person's position. This can help your child better understand his or her own position, or may even make her rethink some things!

Through this activity, your child will be practicing the skills covered by the standard. He or she will present an opinion on a topic and support that opinion with reasons that are bolstered by specific details and evidence. In addition, your child will learn to view a topic in a way he or she may not have considered before.

# ? Quiz

1. The Winter Olympics began in 1924 and have been held in many countries to celebrate sports played on ice and snow. Which Winter Olympic sport is your favorite, and why? Be sure to include reasons and facts to support your choice.

   Which of the following is NOT an example of a good sentence to support your argument?

   A. *Hockey players have to be able to skate and turn quickly while shooting a tiny puck into a net.*

   B. *Snowboarders do amazing jumps and spin high in the air—sometimes even upside down!*

   C. *Cross-country skiers are like marathon runners; they have to ski many miles up and down mountains and through the woods.*

   D. *The United States is good at figure skating.*

2. When you go to your school cafeteria, you probably have some options for what to drink. In addition to milk, juice, and water, some schools want to start offering soda with school lunches. In your opinion, should schools sell soda in cafeterias, and why? Be sure to include reasons and facts to support your choice.

   Which of the following is a strong sentence to support your argument?
   A. *Most sodas have lots of sugar, which means they aren't a very healthy thing to drink, and schools should help their students be as healthy as possible.*
   B. *I like diet soda better than regular.*
   C. *I don't really care since I don't drink soda anyway.*
   D. *My friend Shawn's mom lets him drink soda, so I always drink it at his house because my mom won't buy it for me.*

3. Gym class or physical education is part of the day at most schools, but some people think it takes up time in which students could be learning. In your opinion, should gym class be mandatory at your school, and why? Be sure to include reasons and facts to support your choice.

   Which of the following is NOT an example of a good sentence to support your argument?
   A. *Running around in gym class makes me tired, so it's harder for me to pay attention in class afterward.*
   B. *Sitting in a classroom all day can be boring, so it's nice to have a break to get up and play for a while sometimes.*
   C. *I don't like playing dodgeball because it hurts when I get hit.*
   D. *My gym teacher teaches us things that my classroom teacher doesn't, like how it's important to exercise and be healthy.*

For questions 4 and 5, have your child write a one-paragraph response to the prompts below.

4. Since the late twentieth century, NASA has spent billions of dollars to send rovers to explore the surface of Mars. In your opinion, is it important for NASA to continue sending rovers to Mars, and why? Be sure to include reasons and facts to support your choice.

   _____

   _____

   _____

   _____

   _____

   _____

5. Millions of Americans have at least one pet. Dogs and cats are the most popular, but other animals like birds and fish are popular too. In your opinion, what is the best kind of pet to have, and why? Be sure to include reasons and facts to support your choice.

_____

_____

_____

_____

# ✓ Answers

1. Which of the following is NOT an example of a good sentence to support your argument?

   *The correct answer is D. This sentence doesn't contain enough specific information to provide good support for why figure skating is your favorite Winter Olympic sport. It doesn't say anything about figure skating to convince the reader of your opinion.*

2. Which of the following is a strong sentence to support your argument?

   *The correct answer is A. This is a strong supporting sentence because it contains a lot of specific details about the author's opinion on selling soda in school cafeterias. He states a fact about soda along with how that fact doesn't support his opinion that schools should help their students be healthy.*

3. Which of the following is NOT an example of a good sentence to support your argument?

   *The correct answer is C. This sentence is just a personal opinion about why gym class shouldn't be mandatory. It's not a strong supporting sentence because it doesn't provide any specific information to support this opinion.*

4. Sample Answer:

   *I think it is important for NASA to continue sending rovers to Mars. The rovers collect lots of really important information about Mars that humans wouldn't be able to get themselves. Humans haven't been able to go to Mars yet, so the rovers are our only way to learn about them. The rovers are looking for proof of water on Mars, which means there could be life there too. Learning about life on Mars could help scientists learn about life on Earth.*

5. Sample Answer:

   *Even though I don't have a pet, I think a dog is the best kind of pet to have. Dogs are the easiest kind of pet to play with because they have lots of energy and love to run around and fetch. You can also train dogs to do all kinds of tricks, which I think would be fun to do. But what really makes dogs the best pets is that they can also protect you and your family. Your dog might bark whenever a stranger comes to your door, which helps keep you safe.*

# THE STANDARD

**W.5.5:** *Planning and Revising*
*With guidance and support from peers and adults, develop and strengthen writing as needed by planning, revising, editing, rewriting, or trying a new approach. (Editing for conventions should demonstrate command of Language standards 1-3 up to and including grade 5.)*

## What does it mean?

This writing standard focuses on a child's ability to improve upon his or her writing. The standard includes strategies for planning one's writing, as well as for revising the writing to make it clearer. The standard also focuses on editing for punctuation, spelling, grammar, and other writing conventions. As such, it is closely related to the Conventions of Standard English standards that are part of the Common Core Language skills. The fifth grade standards related to this are highlighted in the sidebar.

**L.5.1:** Demonstrate command of the conventions of standard English grammar and usage when writing or speaking.

- **L.5.1.a:** Explain the function of conjunctions, prepositions, and interjections in general and their function in particular sentences.
- **L.5.1.b:** Form and use the perfect (e.g., *I had walked; I have walked; I will have walked*) verb tenses.
- **L.5.1.c:** Use verb tense to convey various times, sequences, states, and conditions.
- **L.5.1.d:** Recognize and correct inappropriate shifts in verb tense.
- **L.5.1.e:** Use correlative conjunctions (e.g., *either/or, neither/nor*).

**L.5.2:** Demonstrate command of the conventions of standard English capitalization, punctuation, and spelling when writing.

- **L.5.2.a:** Use punctuation to separate items in a series.
- **L.5.2.b:** Use a comma to separate an introductory element from the rest of the sentence.
- **L.5.2.c:** Use a comma to set off the words *yes* and *no* (e.g., *Yes, thank you*), to set off a tag question from the rest of the sentence (e.g., *It's true, isn't it?*), and to indicate direct address (e.g., *Is that you, Steve?*).
- **L.5.2.d:** Use underlining, quotation marks, or italics to indicate titles of works.
- **L.5.2.e:** Spell grade-appropriate words correctly, consulting references as needed,

## Try this together

In the previous lesson, you helped your child plan a piece of writing. This lesson will focus on the revising and editing stages of writing.

Explain that writing involves several steps. The revision process is when a writer looks back at the draft to improve upon it. Revising involves reading it to make sure that the main idea is clearly stated; that there are facts, definitions, and details supporting the main idea; that the organization makes sense; and that there is no extraneous information. Writers should also look for vague or overused words during the revision process to see if they can find other options.

Once all revisions have taken place, the draft is ready to be edited. It is during the editing process that a writer checks to make sure that the grammar, spelling, punctuation, and other language conventions are correct.

A checklist like the one on the following page can help your child revise and edit any piece of writing.

Before your child revises and edits the following paragraph, read through and familiarize yourself with the errors it contains. This will make it easier for you to be of assistance. Encourage your son or daughter to mark the paragraph while looking for ways to improve it. This can be done by circling or underlining certain parts of the text. Also suggest that the paragraph be read through several times to make sure that all errors are caught.

## School Clothes

I agree with my parents that the clothes I wear for school should be totaly different from the cloths I wear for fun. For school, I wearing brown pants a button-down blue shirt and shiney black shoes. When I get home from school, I change into jeans and a T-shirt because I like to play outside and get dirty. in the past, I wore my school clothes outside to play, but my Parents got madd, so I dont do that anymore they said I can either put on play clothes before go outside, or I can play inside insted.

_____

_____

_____

_____

## ✔ Answers

Note that certain revision changes, such as the concluding sentence, will vary from person to person. This exercise requires your child to make revisions and edits based on his or her understanding of clear and appropriate language usage. It also requires your child to understand the basic organization of an argument, with an introductory topic sentence that states an opinion, supporting details in the body, and a concluding sentence that sums up the central idea. Corrected paragraph:

_I agree with my parents that the clothes I wear for school should be totally different from the clothes I wear for fun. For school, I wear brown pants, a button-down blue shirt, and shiny black shoes. When I get home from school, I change into jeans and a T-shirt because_

*I like to play outside and get dirty. In the past, I wore my school clothes outside to play, but my parents got mad, so I don't do that anymore. They said I can either put on play clothes before going outside, or I can play inside instead. In my opinion, wearing different clothes for school and fun makes a lot of sense.*

# Extra practice

To help your child work on the skills assessed by this standard, try this activity:

Sometimes the best way to improve a piece of writing is to change the way you approach the topic. This can involve changing the focus or structure of your piece.

1. Ask your child to write a 1–2 paragraph report on Hurricane Katrina. Make sure he or she focuses on the facts of the disaster, including information on its strength and the damage it caused.

2. Next, ask your child to write another short report on the very same topic. However, for this report, ask your child to concentrate on including eyewitness accounts of the disaster rather than facts.

A new approach to the same topic can result in drastic differences. In some cases, a more fact-based approach would be desirable. In others, a more personal account might give readers a better sense of the human perspective on events. Knowing which approach will work best for your writing is an important part of planning and revising.

| Revising and Editing Checklist | | |
|---|---|---|
| Focus/Ideas | Does the report have a clear topic? | |
| | Does the report stay on topic? | |
| | Does the report have the right approach for the audience who will read it? | |
| Organization | Are the ideas presented in a way that makes sense? | |
| | Are ideas supported by facts, definitions, and details? | |
| Conventions | Have you used correct grammar, such as the appropriate verb tense and subject-verb agreement? | |
| | Is the first word of each sentence capitalized? Are proper nouns (names of people and places) capitalized? | |
| | Is there a period at the end of each sentence? Are commas, quotation marks, question marks, and other punctuation marks used correctly? | |
| | Are all words spelled correctly? | |

# ❓ Quiz

Have your child read the passage and then answer the questions that follow.

(1) I like going to the supermarket _____ my mom lets me pick out things for dinner. (2) Each aisle _____ different things to choose from. (3) Last week, I _____ that I wanted to have taco night, so we bought ground beef, taco shells, and cheese. (4) _____ my sister complained that she doesn't like tacos. (5) Afterward, I told mom I _____ something everyone enjoys from now on.

# ❓ Questions

1. In sentence 1, which word is the best choice to fill the blank?
   A. although                    B. because
   C. unless                      D. despite

2. In sentence 2, which word is the best choice to fill the blank?
   A. did have                    B. was having
   C. will have                   D. has

3. In sentence 3, which word is the best choice to fill the blank?
   A. decide                      B. decided
   C. will decide                 D. did decide

4. In sentence 4, which word is the best choice to fill the blank?
   A. However,                    B. As a result,
   C. Therefore,                  D. Although,

5. In sentence 5, which word is the best choice to fill the blank?
   A. will be choosing            B. choose
   C. would have chosen           D. chose

# ✅ Answers

1. In sentence 1, which word is the best choice to fill the blank?
   *The correct answer is B. "Because" is the conjunction that best retains the meaning of the sentence.*

2. In sentence 2, which word is the best choice to fill the blank?
   *The correct answer is D. The present tense verb is correct in this sentence because this statement is true all of the time. Each aisle of the supermarket will always have different things to choose from.*

3. In sentence 3, which word is the best choice to fill the blank?

   *The correct answer is B. The past tense verb is correct in this sentence because the speaker made the decision in the past ("Last week").*

4. In sentence 4, which word is the best choice to fill the blank?

   *The correct answer is A. The conjunctive adverb "however" is correct because it shows the contrast between the speaker saying he wanted tacos and his sister saying that she didn't.*

5. In sentence 5, which word is the best choice to fill the blank?

   *The correct answer is A. The future progressive tense verb is correct in this sentence because it shows that the speaker will continue to choose in the future, more than once.*

MATHEMATICS

# OVERVIEW

For Grade 5, the Mathematics Common Core Standards focus heavily on three skill areas. The first skill area is understanding place value and decimals, using models to illustrate. This also covers utilizing decimals in division operations and applying these skills in measurement conversions. The second skill area is fractions, which covers handling fractions with unlike denominators, as well as multiplication and division of fractions. The third skill area focuses on understanding the concept of volume and finding the volume of rectangular prisms.

Listed below are the Mathematics Common Core Standards for Grade 5 that we have identified as "power standards." We consider these standards to be critical for the success for your child. Each lesson in this section focuses on a single standard (or set of related standards) so that you and your child may practice that specific skill to achieve mastery. The applicable standards are divided into three categories: Number & Operations in Base Ten; Number & Operations—Fractions; and Measurement & Data.

## Number & Operations in Base Ten

### 1. The Place Value System

**CCSS.Math.Content.5.NBT.A.1:** Recognize that in a multi-digit number, a digit in one place represents 10 times as much as it represents in the place to its right and $\frac{1}{10}$ of what it represents in the place to its left.

**CCSS.Math.Content.5.NBT.A.2:** Explain patterns in the number of zeros of the product when multiplying a number by powers of 10, and explain patterns in the placement of the decimal point when a decimal is multiplied or divided by a power of 10. Use whole-number exponents to denote powers of 10.

*CCSS.Math.Content.5.NBT.A.3:* Read, write, and compare decimals to thousandths.

*CCSS.Math.Content.5.NBT.A.3a:* Read and write decimals to thousandths using base-ten numerals, number names, and expanded form, e.g., $347.392 = 3 \times 100 + 4 \times 10 + 7 \times 1 + 3 \times \left(\dfrac{1}{10}\right) + 9 \times \left(\dfrac{1}{100}\right) + 2 \times \left(\dfrac{1}{1000}\right)$.

*CCSS.Math.Content.5.NBT.A.3b:* Compare two decimals to thousandths based on meanings of the digits in each place, using $>$, $=$, and $<$ symbols to record the results of comparisons.

*CCSS.Math.Content.5.NBT.A.4:* Use place value understanding to round decimals to any place.

## 2. Division with Area Models

*CCSS.Math.Content.5.NBT.B.6:* Find whole-number quotients of whole numbers with up to four-digit dividends and two-digit divisors, using strategies based on place value, the properties of operations, and/or the relationship between multiplication and division. Illustrate and explain the calculation by using equations, rectangular arrays, and/or area models.

## 3. Division with Properties of Operations and Place Value

*CCSS.Math.Content.5.NBT.B.6:* Find whole-number quotients of whole numbers with up to four-digit dividends and two-digit divisors, using strategies based on place value, the properties of operations, and/or the relationship between multiplication and division. Illustrate and explain the calculation by using equations, rectangular arrays, and/or area models.

## 4. Operations with Decimals

*CCSS.Math.Content.5.NBT.B.7:* Add, subtract, multiply, and divide decimals to hundredths, using concrete models or drawings and strategies based on place value, properties of operations, and/or the relationship between addition and subtraction; relate the strategy to a written method and explain the reasoning used.

## 5. Multi-Step Problems (includes Measurement & Data)

*CCSS.Math.Content.5.NBT.B.6:* Find whole-number quotients of whole numbers with up to four-digit dividends and two-digit divisors, using strategies based on place value, the properties of operations, and/or the relationship between multiplication and division. Illustrate and explain the calculation by using equations, rectangular arrays, and/or area models.

***CCSS.Math.Content.5.NBT.B.7:*** Add, subtract, multiply, and divide decimals to hundredths, using concrete models or drawings and strategies based on place value, properties of operations, and/or the relationship between addition and subtraction; relate the strategy to a written method and explain the reasoning used.

***CCSS.Math.Content.5.MD.A.1:*** Convert among different-sized standard measurement units within a given measurement system (e.g., convert 5 cm to 0.05 m), and use these conversions in solving multi-step, real world problems.

# Number & Operations—Fractions

## 6. Adding and Subtracting Fractions

***CCSS.Math.Content.5.NF.A.1:*** Add and subtract fractions with unlike denominators (including mixed numbers) by replacing given fractions with equivalent fractions in such a way as to produce an equivalent sum or difference of fractions with like denominators. For example, $\frac{2}{3} + \frac{5}{4} = \frac{8}{12} + \frac{15}{12} = \frac{23}{12}$. (In general, $\frac{a}{b} + \frac{c}{d} = \frac{(ad+bc)}{bd}$.)

***CCSS.Math.Content.5.NF.A.2:*** Solve word problems involving addition and subtraction of fractions referring to the same whole, including cases of unlike denominators, e.g., by using visual fraction models or equations to represent the problem. Use benchmark fractions and number sense of fractions to estimate mentally and assess the reasonableness of answers. For example, recognize an incorrect result $\frac{2}{5} + \frac{1}{2} = \frac{3}{7}$, by observing that $\frac{3}{7} < \frac{1}{2}$.

## 7. Multiplying Fractions

***CCSS.Math.Content.5.NF.B.4:*** Apply and extend previous understandings of multiplication to multiply a fraction or whole number by a fraction.

***CCSS.Math.Content.5.NF.B.4a:*** Interpret the product $\left(\frac{a}{b}\right) \times q$ as a parts of a partition of $q$ into $b$ equal parts; equivalently, as the result of a sequence of operations $a \times q \div b$. For example, use a visual fraction model to show (2/3) × 4 = 8/3, and create a story context for this equation. Do the same with (2/3) × (4/5) = 8/15. (In general, $\left(\frac{a}{b}\right) \times \left(\frac{c}{d}\right) = \frac{ac}{bd}$.)

**CCSS.Math.Content.5.NF.B.6:** Solve real world problems involving multiplication of fractions and mixed numbers, e.g., by using visual fraction models or equations to represent the problem.

## 8. Exploring Fraction Multiplication

**CCSS.Math.Content.5.NF.B.4b:** Find the area of a rectangle with fractional side lengths by tiling it with unit squares of the appropriate unit fraction side lengths, and show that the area is the same as would be found by multiplying the side lengths. Multiply fractional side lengths to find areas of rectangles, and represent fraction products as rectangular areas.

**CCSS.Math.Content.5.NF.B.5b:** Explaining why multiplying a given number by a fraction greater than 1 results in a product greater than the given number (recognizing multiplication by whole numbers greater than 1 as a familiar case); explaining why multiplying a given number by a fraction less than 1 results in a product smaller than the given number; and relating the principle of fraction equivalence $\frac{a}{b} = \frac{(n \times a)}{(n \times b)}$ to the effect of multiplying $\frac{a}{b}$ by 1.

## 9. Dividing Fractions

**CCSS.Math.Content.5.NF.B.7:** Apply and extend previous understandings of division to divide unit fractions by whole numbers and whole numbers by unit fractions.1

**CCSS.Math.Content.5.NF.B.7a:** Interpret division of a unit fraction by a non-zero whole number, and compute such quotients. For example, create a story context for $\left(\frac{1}{3}\right) \div 4$, and use a visual fraction model to show the quotient. Use the relationship between multiplication and division to explain that $\left(\frac{1}{3}\right) \div 4 = \frac{1}{12}$ because $\left(\frac{1}{12}\right) \times 4 = \frac{1}{3}$.

**CCSS.Math.Content.5.NF.B.7b:** Interpret division of a whole number by a unit fraction, and compute such quotients. For example, create a story context for $4 \div \left(\frac{1}{5}\right)$, and use a visual fraction model to show the quotient. Use the relationship between multiplication and division to explain that $4 \div \left(\frac{1}{5}\right) = 20$ because $20 \times \left(\frac{1}{5}\right) = 4$.

**CCSS.Math.Content.5.NF.B.7c:** Solve real world problems involving division of unit fractions by non-zero whole numbers and division of whole numbers by unit fractions, e.g., by using visual fraction models and equations to represent the problem. For example, how much chocolate will each person get if 3 people share $\frac{1}{2}$ lb of chocolate equally? How many $\frac{1}{3}$-cup servings are in 2 cups of raisins?

# Measurement & Data

## 10. Volume

***CCSS.Math.Content.5.MD.C.4:*** Measure volumes by counting unit cubes, using cubic cm, cubic in, cubic ft, and improvised units.

***CCSS.Math.Content.5.MD.C.5:*** Relate volume to the operations of multiplication and addition and solve real world and mathematical problems involving volume.

***CCSS.Math.Content.5.MD.C.5a:*** Find the volume of a right rectangular prism with whole-number side lengths by packing it with unit cubes, and show that the volume is the same as would be found by multiplying the edge lengths, equivalently by multiplying the height by the area of the base. Represent threefold whole-number products as volumes, e.g., to represent the associative property of multiplication.

***CCSS.Math.Content.5.MD.C.5b:*** Apply the formulas $V = l \times w \times h$ and $V = b \times h$ for rectangular prisms to find volumes of right rectangular prisms with whole-number edge lengths in the context of solving real world and mathematical problems.

***CCSS.Math.Content.5.MD.C.5c:*** Recognize volume as additive. Find volumes of solid figures composed of two non-overlapping right rectangular prisms by adding the volumes of the non-overlapping parts, applying this technique to solve real world problems.

# THE STANDARDS

**5.NBT.A.1:** *Recognize that in a multi-digit number, a digit in one place represents 10 times as much as it represents in the place to its right and $\frac{1}{10}$ of what it represents in the place to its left.*

**5.NBT.A.2:** *Explain patterns in the number of zeros of the product when multiplying a number by powers of 10, and explain patterns in the placement of the decimal point when a decimal is multiplied or divided by a power of 10. Use whole-number exponents to denote powers of 10.*

**5.NBT.A.3:** *Read, write, and compare decimals to thousandths.*

**5.NBT.A.3a:** *Read and write decimals to thousandths using base-ten numerals, number names, and expanded form, e.g., $347.392 = 3 \times 100 + 4 \times 10 + 7 \times 1 + 3 \times \left(\frac{1}{10}\right) + 9 \times \left(\frac{1}{100}\right) + 2 \times \left(\frac{1}{1000}\right)$.*

**5.NBT.A.3b:** *Compare two decimals to thousandths based on meanings of the digits in each place, using >, =, and < symbols to record the results of comparisons.*

**5.NBT.A.4:** *Use place value understanding to round decimals to any place.*

## What does it mean?

In fourth grade, students learned how to name, expand, and compare whole numbers using place value. They also observed the effects of multiplying or dividing by 10 or 100. In fifth grade they will use the same skills, but expand them to decimals.

## Try this together

These standards represent the culmination of students' understanding of place value. There are four major concepts represented here.

Prior to 5th grade, students were expected to understand how place value works for whole numbers. By now, your child should have a clear understanding that each place is ten times as large as the one to its right. Therefore, 300 is ten times as much as 30, which is ten times as large as 3. In 5th grade, that thinking extends to decimals: 3 is ten times as large as 0.3, which is ten times as large as 0.03, which is ten times as large as 0.003. Similarly, we can reverse this thinking: 0.007 is one tenth of 0.07, which is one tenth of 0.7, etc.

Your child should come into fifth grade already knowing how to write whole numbers in expanded form. For example, 5,482 can be written as $5 \times 1{,}000 + 4 \times 100 + 8 \times 10 + 2 \times 1$. A new expectation in 5th grade is understanding that the numbers 1,000, 100, and 10 are all *powers of 10*. That means they can be written in exponential form: $1{,}000 = 10^3$, $100 = 10^2$, and $10 = 10^1$. (In middle school, your child will learn about zero and negative exponents, which will be used for other place value problems.)

It is also important at this point for your child to recognize that there is a pattern when multiplying a number by a power of ten: $6 \times 10^5 = 600{,}000$ and $25 \times 10^2 = 2{,}500$. When multiplying by a power of ten, the power tells you how many digits will follow the original number in the final product. When multiplying a decimal by a power of ten, we do not simply attach more zeros to the end of the number. Instead, we move the decimal point, because moving the decimal point changes the place value of each digit. The number 16.59 is ten times as large as 1.659, because each digit is shifted one place to the left. So to multiply $5.873 \times 100$, simply move the decimal to the right two times to make each digit 100 times larger: $5.873 \times 100 = 587.3$.

When dividing decimals by powers of ten, move the decimal point to the left the appropriate number of times to make each digit's place value smaller: $598.42 \div 100 = 5.9842$.

The next big idea about place value is being able to write, name, and expand decimal numbers in base ten. Your child should already know how to read whole numbers—for example, 4,873 is "four thousand, eight hundred seventy-three." To extend this to decimals, your child will need to know that the first digit to the right of the decimal point represents *tenths*, the second represents *hundredths*, and the third represents *thousandths*. So 55.7 can be read "fifty-five and seven tenths;" 48.09 is "forty-eight and nine hundredths;" and 72.003 is "seventy-two and three thousandths." When there are several non-zero digits after the decimal, we usually read it with reference to the smallest digit. Therefore 93.592 is "ninety-three and five hundred ninety-two thousandths."

Another way to represent a decimal is in standard is expanded form. In 4th grade, your child most likely learned to write whole numbers in expanded form. Now we are extending this to decimals, using the fractions $\frac{1}{10}$, $\frac{1}{100}$, and $\frac{1}{1000}$. For example, 689.351 would be expanded as

$$6 \times 100 + 8 \times 10 + 9 \times 1 + 3 \times \frac{1}{10} + 5 \times \frac{1}{100} + 1 \times \frac{1}{1000}.$$

Along the same lines, your child will need to be able to compare two decimal numbers using > ("greater than"), < ("less than"), or = ("equal to"). Your child should already have a good foundation using these symbols to compare whole numbers from previous grades. Similar to whole numbers, decimals can be compared by finding the greatest place value where they have different numbers, and seeing which is greater. Thus $53.802 > 53.715$ because the first number that is different is the tenths digit, and 53.802 has more tenths (8) than 53.715 (which has 7).

Students often struggle when asked to compare decimals that have different numbers of digits past the decimal place, such as 12.317 and 12.9. The first number may seem larger because 317 is more than 9. But this is misleading. 12.317 only has a little more than 3 tenths, while 12.9 has 9 tenths. Therefore $12.317 < 12.9$.

The last aspect of place value that comes up in 5th grade is rounding. In earlier grades, your child should have already learned how to round whole numbers—for example, 347 to the nearest ten is 350. Now she will be rounding decimals to decimal place values: 68.93 to the nearest whole is 69. To the nearest tenth, it is 68.9. The number 134,780.913 to the nearest tenth is 134,780.913.

This is a time when your child's prior knowledge will be very important. If she has not mastered place value at the 4th-grade level (which requires all the same techniques these standards require, but for whole numbers only) then she will certainly have trouble here. Take some time to ask questions about whole number place value. Does your child understand that thousands are ten times as big as hundreds, and hundreds are ten times as big as tens? Does she know how to expand a whole number into its place value parts?

One of the simplest things you can do is ask your child to do some quick mental math, multiplying and dividing numbers by 10, 100, or 1,000. Start out simple, but give her lots of opportunities to practice.

You can illustrate place value in decimals whenever you are out shopping. Next time you use cash, ask your child to expand the change into its place value. 46 cents is $4 \times \frac{1}{10} + 6 \times \frac{1}{100}$. If she has trouble with this concept, practice making change using only dimes (tenths) and pennies (hundredths). Also ask her to round—round the change to the nearest tenth of a dollar, or to the nearest dollar. Help her see that rounding to the nearest tenth of a dollar is the same as rounding to the nearest ten cents.

Comparing decimals is probably the most difficult part of this whole concept. Again, stick to money. Which is more, 0.80 or 0.08? What if you write 0.8 instead of 0.80? You'd be surprised how many students think that 0.5 dollars is the same as 5 cents!

**Quiz**

1. In the number 4,134.1, how many times greater is the first 1 than the second 1?

2. Solve each problem and explain how you know the answer:
   a) 35 × 1,000                      b) 6,840 ÷ 100

3. Write the number 5,804.531 in expanded form and in words.

4. Fill in the blanks with <, >, or =. Explain why you chose the symbol you chose.
   a) 24.94 ___ 24.84         b) 563.80 ___ 563.8         c) 795.624 ___ 795.7

5. Round 7,904.652 to the nearest...
   a) tenth                      b) hundred                      c) ten
   d) hundredth                  e) whole

 **Answers**

*1. In the number 4,134.1, how much larger is the first 1 than the second 1?*
   *It is 1,000 times larger, because it is 3 places to the left. 0.1 × 1,000 = 100.*
   *This question assesses your child's understanding of the relative size of the places in a base-ten number. Does your child understand that each place to the left is ten times larger than the place to its immediate right?*

2. Solve each problem and explain how you know the answer:

   a) 35 × 1,000

   b) 6,840 ÷ 100

   *For a, the answer is 35,000. You are multiplying by 1,000, which is like multiplying by 10 three times ($10^3$). Each factor of 10 requires us to attach another 0 to the end of the whole number, increasing each digit's place value by one place.*

   *For b, the answer is 68.4. This is a tricky one, because you are dividing a multiple of 10 (that is, a whole number that ends in a 0) twice. The first time you divide by 10, you shift the digits to the right by removing the final 0, giving 684. Dividing by another 10 moves the decimal point one place to the left (or the digits one more place to the right), giving 68.4. Another way to think of it is to add a decimal point to the end of 6,840, after the ones place, where it belongs. Then move the decimal point two places to the left.*

   *This question assesses your child's understanding of multiplication and division by powers of ten. In a), your child should understand that solving this problem is simply a matter of attaching more zeroes to the end of the number, to make it larger. For b, division is a tougher concept for many students, and there is a twist in this problem, which requires your child to both remove a final zero and move the decimal point, turning a whole number into a decimal.*

3. Write the number 5,804.531 in expanded form and in words.

   *The expanded form is $5 \times 1,000 + 8 \times 100 + 0 \times 10 + 4 \times 1 + 5 \times \dfrac{1}{10} + 3 \times \dfrac{1}{100} + 1 \times \dfrac{1}{1000}$. The name of this number is five thousand, eight hundred four and five hundred thirty-one thousandths.*

   *This problem is straightforward practice with expanded form and naming numbers.*

4. Fill in the blanks with <, >, or =. Explain why you chose the symbol you chose.

   a) 24.84 ___ 24.89

   b) 563.80 ___ 563.8

   c) 795.624 ___ 795.7

   *For a, the numbers are the same until the hundredths place, where 9 hundredths is greater than 4 hundredths. The answer is <.*

   *For b, these numbers are equal (=). The first number has 80 hundredths, and the second has 8 tenths, which are equivalent fractions ($\dfrac{80}{100} = \dfrac{8}{10}$). The only difference in the decimals is an additional zero to the right of the final non-zero digit, which does not change the value of the number—in fact, you could write many more zeros, and it still would not change the value of the number. Your child may be misled by the fact that 80 is larger than*

*8. In that case, remind her to focus on the place value of each individual digit. In both of these numbers, the 8 represents 8 tenths.*

*For c, these numbers differ first in the tenths place, where the first number has 6 tenths and the second has 7 tenths. Even though 624 is greater than 7 as whole numbers, 0.624 is less than 0.7. The answer is <.*

*This question assesses your child's ability to compare decimal numbers, with two trickier example in b and c that highlight areas that often confuse students.*

5. Round 7,904.652 to the nearest...

    a) tenth      b) hundred      c) ten

    d) hundredth     e) whole

*The answers are:*

*a) 7.904.7; when the digit to the right of the place being rounded to is 5 or more, round up.*

*b) 7,900; the tens digit is 0, so round down.*

*c) 7,900; the ones digit is 4, so round down. It is interesting that this gives the same value as rounding to the nearest hundred.*

*d) 7,904.65; the thousandths digit is 2, so round down.*

*e) 7,905; the tenths digit is 6, so round up.*

*This is a straightforward rounding question. The important things are being able to identify which place value should be the final digit in the answer, and deciding whether to round up or down. Point out to your child the importance of the –th ending in numbers to the right of the decimal point.*

# THE STANDARD

*5.NBT.B.6: Find whole-number quotients of whole numbers with up to four-digit dividends and two-digit divisors, using strategies based on place value, the properties of operations, and/or the relationship between multiplication and division. Illustrate and explain the calculation by using equations, rectangular arrays, and/or area models.*

## What does it mean?

This standard addresses division with large whole numbers—up to four-digit numbers divided by two-digit numbers. The standard proposes a variety of different strategies for students to use for division, which we will cover in this lesson and Lesson 3. In this lesson, we will use area models as a tool for finding quotients. Your child is likely familiar with area models from multiplication problems. An area model shows a multiplication or division problem with a geometric representation. For example, $5 \times 4 = 20$ can be shown as a rectangle with dimensions 5 and 4, and an area of 20.

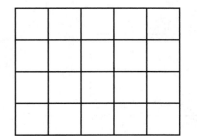

Area model
for $5 \times 4 = 20$

## Try this together

To help your child master the area model, ask him to answer questions about rectangles, where the area and one dimension are known, and the other dimension is required. Start with small, familiar numbers. For example:

*How long is a rectangle with an area of 20, whose width is 2?*

Using area models for multiplication, he should realize that the unknown dimension must be 10, because $10 \times 2 = 20$. Remember that the area of a rectangle is its *length × width*. You can also turn it into a contextual problem by using any rectangle you see:

*A kitchen window is 3 feet tall, and has an area of 6 square feet. How wide is the window?*

Questions like these are a great way to help your child begin to think of division in terms of area. If the area is 6 square feet, and the height is 3 feet, your child should be able to visualize a window made up of 6 squares, stacked 3 units high, giving the window a width of 2 feet, as shown below.

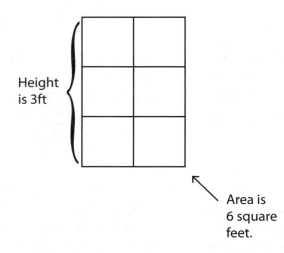

Height is 3ft

Area is 6 square feet.

In fourth grade, children learned how to multiply using area models. This area model shows 32 × 58, by thinking of the length as 3 tens + 2 ones and the width as 5 tens + 8 ones. Because the area of the whole rectangle equals the area of each of the smaller rectangles added together, the total area is 1,500 + 100 + 240 + 16 = 1,856.

|  | 50 (5 tens) | 8 (8 ones) |
|---|---|---|
| 30 (3 tens) | 3 tens × 5 tens<br>= 15 hundreds = 1,500 | 3 tens × 8 =<br>24 tens = 240 |
| 2 (2 ones) | 2 × 5 tens = 10 tens = 100 | 8 × 2 = 16 |

In the window problem above, you used the area (6 square feet) and the height (3 feet) of the window to find its width by using multiplication in reverse: division. In the same way, you can use area models for multi-digit numbers to solve division problems by multiplying in reverse.

Let's take the window problem from earlier, and ask the same question, but in inches instead of feet:

*A kitchen window is 36 inches tall, and has an area of 864 square inches. How wide is the window?*

To solve this, your child should use a more complex area model that uses place value. The height of the window is 36 inches, but it can be easier to think of this as 30 inches + 6 inches or 3 tens and 6 ones, as shown on the model.

To find the width, start by looking for a number in the tens place that can be multiplied by 30 + 6 without exceeding 865. The number 20 (2 tens) can be multiplied by 30 to get 600 and by 6 to get 120. This accounts for 600 + 120 = 720 square inches, which is close to 864 but not too much.

This leaves 864 − 720 = 144 square inches left to account for by multiplying 30 + 6 by a number in the ones place. The number 4 (which is 4 ones) can be multiplied by 30 to get 120 and by 6 to get 24. The total area is 120 + 24 = 144.

Thus, (30 + 6) × (20 + 4) = 864, so you know that 864 ÷ 36 = 24. Reinforce that the number inside each smaller rectangle refers to the area of that rectangle, and that the area of the whole rectangle is the sum of all of the smaller areas.

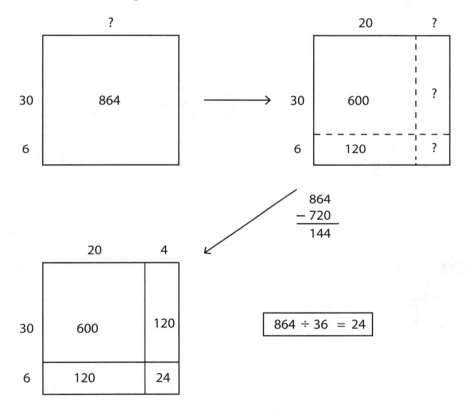

In solving a problem like this, your child may need several attempts at guess and check. If he first tries 30, instead of 20, then the area will come out too large, and he will need to adjust. That is perfectly normal—it is an expectation of this standard.

Below are a few examples of the kinds of problems this standard will require your child to solve. Remember that there are lots of ways to solve a division problem. As you work through these problems with your child, use an area model for each one in order to help your child become proficient with that representation.

**? Quiz**

1. Which of the following shows the correct first step in using an area model to solve 3,266 ÷ 46?

A)
<br>8
<br>40
<br>6

B)
<br>80
<br>40
<br>6

C)
<br>7
<br>40
<br>6

D)
<br>70
<br>40
<br>6

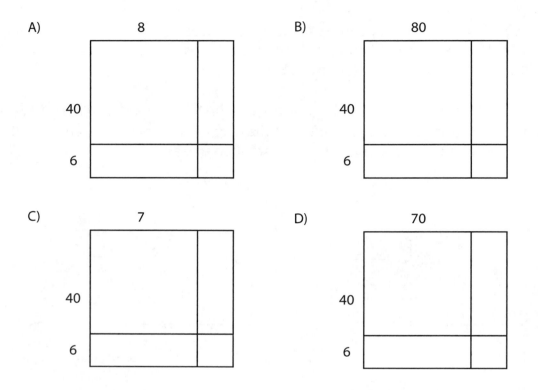

2. Complete the area model to find 931 ÷ 7 = ?

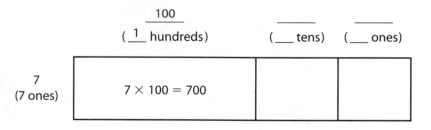

3. Complete the area model to find 368 ÷ 16 = ?

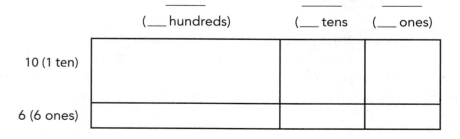

4. Use an area model to find 4,067 ÷ 49 = ?

5. The soccer field at a local park is 95 yards long. The area of the field is 6,080 square yards. How wide is the field? Use an area model to show your work.

 **Answers**

1. Which of the following shows the correct first step in using an area model to solve 3,266 ÷ 46?

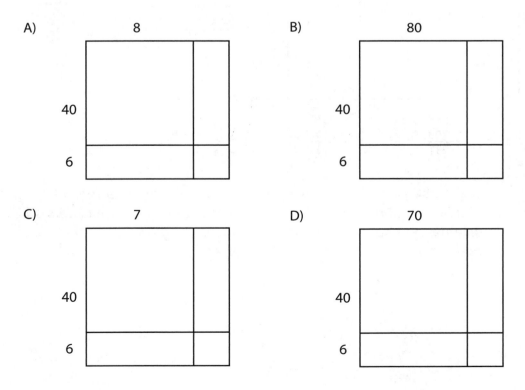

A)  8  40  6

B)  80  40  6

C)  7  40  6

D)  70  40  6

*The correct answer is D. 70 is the correct number of tens in the quotient. If your child chose a different answer, ask him to complete the area model for his answer choice, and see if it leads to a correct quotient, which should be 71.*

*This is an error analysis question, which may help your child understand the area model method for division a little better. If your child is struggling with the guess-and-check process involved in using area models, take a moment to discuss each of the incorrect answers to this problem, and help your child see why they are incorrect.*

2. Complete the area model to find $931 \div 7 = ?$

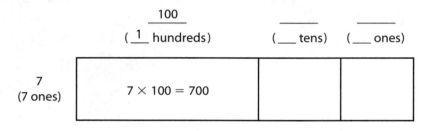

*The correct answer is 133. The area model should look like this:*

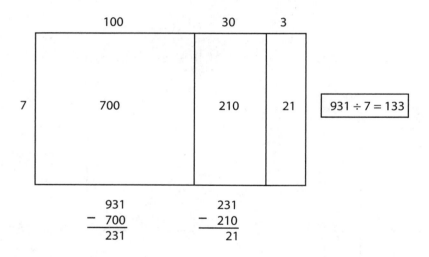

*Questions 2–4 ask your child to perform division using an area models for problems of increasing difficulty, and with less support in each step. If your child gets stuck on any of these problems, remind her that a certain amount of guess and check is necessary for division, and practice with slightly simpler problems.*

3. Complete the area model to find 368 ÷ 16 = ?

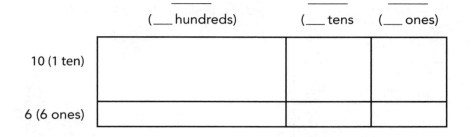

(__ hundreds)   (__ tens)   (__ ones)

10 (1 ten)

6 (6 ones)

*The correct answer is 23. The area model should look like this:*

4. Use an area model to find 4,067 ÷ 49 = ?

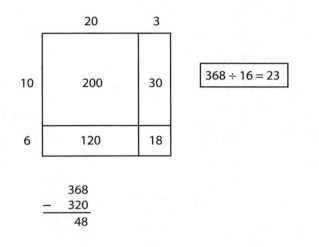

|  | 20 | 3 |
|---|---|---|
| 10 | 200 | 30 |
| 6 | 120 | 18 |

368 ÷ 16 = 23

```
   368
 − 320
   ───
    48
```

*The correct answer is 83. The area model should look like this:*

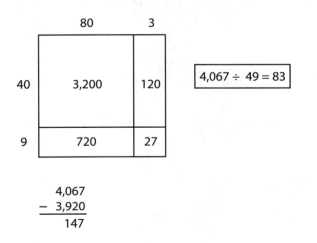

|  | 80 | 3 |
|---|---|---|
| 40 | 3,200 | 120 |
| 9 | 720 | 27 |

4,067 ÷ 49 = 83

```
   4,067
 − 3,920
   ─────
     147
```

5. The soccer field at a local park is 95 yards long. The area of the field is 6,080 square yards. How wide is the field?

*The correct answer is 64 yards. The area model should look like this:*

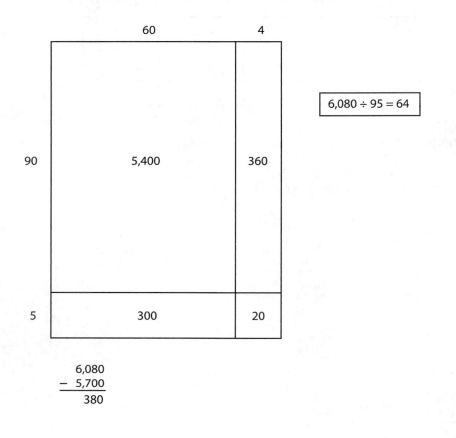

$6,080 \div 95 = 64$

```
  6,080
− 5,700
    380
```

*Question 5 is similar to Questions 2 – 4, but with a context added. For many students, the context may make it easier to create the area model, because it has a tangible meaning.*

# DIVISION: WITH PROPERTIES OF OPERATIONS AND PLACE VALUE

 ## THE STANDARD

**5.NBT.B.6:** *Find whole-number quotients of whole numbers with up to four-digit dividends and two-digit divisors, using strategies based on place value, the properties of operations, and/or the relationship between multiplication and division. Illustrate and explain the calculation by using equations, rectangular arrays, and/or area models.*

## What does it mean?

This standard addresses division with large whole numbers—up to four-digit numbers divided by two-digit numbers. The standard proposes a variety of different strategies for students to use for division, some of which we covered in Lesson 2. In this lesson, we will use the properties of operations and place value. When we talk about properties of operations, we are referring to the fact that division and multiplication are inverse operations. Therefore, if your child already knows how to multiply with whole numbers of a certain size, then the next step is to reverse that thinking to make it work for division. Place value is another useful tool for division. The old-fashioned long division algorithm is based on place value, but students now have access to other methods that are more intuitive.

## Try this together

By now, your child most likely understands that a multiplication equation can be reversed to turn into a division equation. For example, $9 \times 6 = 54$ can be reversed to say either $54 \div 9 = 6$ or $54 \div 6 = 9$. Now we are doing the same process, but with larger numbers. Suppose your child needs to divide 3,472 by 31. She could start by thinking of it as a multiplication problem, with an unknown factor: $31 \times ? = 3,472$. Using what she already knows about place value, your child may be able to estimate that the answer will be something a little larger than 100, because $31 \times 100 = 3,100$, which is close to 3,472.

Encourage your child to begin any division problem with this kind of thinking: first, turning it into a multiplication problem, and then estimating what the missing factor might be based on the size of the numbers. You'd be surprised how close this method will get you most of the time, and how quickly this practice will help your child develop strong number sense.

Of course, in most problems, an exact answer will be required. Let's continue with the same problem, using 100 as our starting point. We already know that $100 \times 31 = 3,100$.

If we subtract 3,472 − 3,100 = 372, then we know we need to find out how many times 31 goes into 372. Again, we can use place value: 10 × 31 = 310, which is pretty close. Looking at what's left, 372 − 310 = 62 and 31 goes into 62 twice with nothing left over. We multiplied 31 by 100 to get 3,100, then by 10 to get 310, and by 2 to get 62. Add them all together: 100 + 10 + 2 = 112. Therefore, 31 × 112 = 3,472, so 3,472 ÷ 31 = 112.

Some students like to show this type of thinking using the "Big 7" algorithm, which organizes the process we just followed:

```
31 | 3472
    - 3100 | 100
      372
    -  310 | 10
       62
    -   62 | 2
        0
```

Here is another example of a Big 7, for 2,378 ÷ 82:

```
82 | 2378
   -  820 | 10
     1558
   -  820 | 10
      738
   -  410 | 5
      328
   -  328 | 4
        0
```

In this example, we are looking for how many times 82 goes into 2,378. The Big 7 allows students to make a sequence of approximations, often using their understanding of place value. The first approximation is 10. 10 × 82 is 820, which we subtract from 2,378, leaving 1,558. We can subtract another 820 from 1,558, so we write another 10. That leaves 738. 5 × 82 is 410, so we subtract 410 from 738, leaving 328, which is 4 × 82. The quotient is the sum of 10 + 10 + 5 + 4, or 29. 2,378 ÷ 82 = 29. The nice thing about the Big 7 method is that you can use as many steps as you need. Some people might start this problem by multiplying by 20, instead of 10. Others may start with 5, or 12, or 25. It doesn't matter what number you start with, as long as you don't go over the total of 2,378. But even if you do, you can always start over with a smaller guess.

# ? Quiz

1. Estimate the quotient of 2,713 ÷ 87.

2. Use a "Big 7" model to solve 598 ÷ 13. Show your work.

3. Solve 1,584 ÷ 24 by using estimation in steps.

4. Solve 8,375 ÷ 67. Show your work.

5. Find the value of *m* for the following equation:
   28 × *m* = 1,204

## Answers

1. *Estimate the quotient of 2,713 ÷ 87.*

   *An estimate of around 30 is ideal here. Because 87 is close to 90 and 90 × 3 = 270, our quotient is going to be close to 30.*

   *Estimation is a great way for your child to become proficient at using place value to solve problems. Pay attention to how your child is solving this problem. When presented with a problem like this, some students are tempted to find an exact answer, either by hand or with a calculator, and then round it to a clean number. That is not the point of estimation—the point is to reason quickly to come up with an answer that is close, when precision is not completely necessary.*

2. *Use a "Big 7" model to solve 598 ÷ 13. Show your work.*

   *The quotient is 46. One possible solution, using the Big 7 method is pictured below. Remember that there are lots of ways to solve a division problem.*

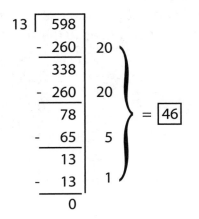

3. Solve 1,584 ÷ 24 by using estimation in steps.

*The quotient is 66. One possible solution, where 1,584 is decomposed, is below.*

| 1,584 | = | 1,000 | + | 500 | + | 80 | + | 4 |
|---|---|---|---|---|---|---|---|---|
| Try 24 × 40 | = | 960 | | | | | | |
| Subtract | | 40 | + | 500 | + | 80 | + | 4 |
| Add the tens | | | | 500 | + | 120 | + | 4 |
| Try 24 × 20 | | | | 480 | | | | |
| Subtract | | | | 20 | + | 120 | + | 4 |

*At this point, you may recognize that 20 + 4 = 24, so that's 1 × 24. You may also notice that 120 = 5 × 24, but if you don't, you could try 2, 3, or 4. Altogether, we have 40 + 20 + 5 + 1 = 66.*

*Problems 2 and 3 both invite your child to try different methods to solve multi-digit division problem. Encourage your child to become familiar with a variety of methods, as each method she masters will help her become more fluent with calculations.*

4. Solve 8,375 ÷ 67. Show your work.

*The quotient is 125. Your child can use this problem to choose the method that he prefers. One method might follow these steps: 67 × 100 = 6,700, so 8,375 − 6,700 = 1,675 remains. In the tens place, 67 × 20 = 1,340, which leaves 1,675 − 1,340 = 335. Finally, 67 × 5 = 335. So, the quotient is 100 + 20 + 5 = 125.*

*This problem invites your child to choose a method that makes the most sense to him. Discuss why he likes the method he chose and when he might use other models.*

5. Find the value of *m* for the following equation:

28 × *m* = 1,204

*The answer is m = 43. Multiplication with a missing factor is another way of writing division, so this problem could also be written as 1,204 ÷ 28 = m.*

*This problem explores two more challenging ideas: division as the reverse of multiplication, and using a letter to represent an unknown number. Both of these concepts should be review from third and fourth grade, but now they are being used in the context of multi-digit division.*

# THE STANDARD

**5.NBT.B.7:** *Add, subtract, multiply, and divide decimals to hundredths, using concrete models or drawings and strategies based on place value, properties of operations, and/or the relationship between addition and subtraction; relate the strategy to a written method and explain the reasoning used.*

## What does it mean?

Grade 5 is the first time your child will be exposed to operations with decimals. At this point, he will only be dealing with decimals to hundredths, the place that is two digits to the right of the decimal point. In prior years, your child likely learned to add, subtract, multiply, and divide with whole numbers. The same methods that worked then will continue to work when dealing with decimals, but with some subtle differences. Place value will be an important tool, particularly for addition and subtraction problems. The same visual models that work for whole numbers will also be useful for decimals. And as always, understanding the inverse nature of addition/subtraction and multiplication/division will be essential to your child's mastery of all four operations.

## Try this together

Decimals can be added or subtracted without much trouble if you break each number into its place value components. To take a simple example, try adding 3.6 + 4.2.

$$3.6 = 3 + \frac{6}{10}$$

$$4.2 = 4 + \frac{2}{10}$$

To add these together, we are really adding 3 wholes to 4 wholes, and 6 tenths to 2 tenths. Therefore, we will have 7 wholes and 8 tenths, or $7\frac{8}{10} = 7.8$.

Sometimes the sum at one place value will be larger than 10. Years ago, we used to talk about "carrying the 1," but this concept is now presented to students in a more conceptual way. For example, to add 27.9 + 31.5 think of:

$$(20 + 7 + \frac{9}{10}) + (30 + 1 + \frac{5}{10}) = 20 + 30 + 7 + 1 + \frac{9}{10} + \frac{5}{10} = 50 + 8 + \frac{14}{10}$$

Notice that 5 tenths + 9 tenths equals 14 tenths, so 10 of those tenths can be combined to make 1 whole:

$$50 + 8 + \frac{14}{10} = 50 + 8 + \frac{10}{10} + \frac{4}{10} = 50 + 8 + 1 + \frac{4}{10} = 50 + 9 + 0.4 = 59.4$$

Notice that whenever you have more than 10 of any place, you can convert 10 of them to 1 unit in the next largest place. For example, 10 tens equals 1 hundred, while 10 hundredths ($\frac{10}{100}$) equals 1 tenth ($\frac{1}{10}$ or 0.1).

The same techniques can be used in subtraction. Let's try 92.6 − 57.8 using a vertical model:

$$90 + 2 + \frac{6}{10}$$
$$- \left( 50 + 7 + \frac{8}{10} \right)$$
$$\overline{\phantom{xxxxxxxxxxxx}}$$

Here is where your child will be able to make sense of the old idea of "borrowing." Starting from the right, we see that 8 tenths is greater than 6 tenths, so it cannot be subtracted. If 1 whole is borrowed from the ones place, it can be written as 10 tenths, giving us a total of 16 tenths. So we can change the way we have 92.6 written, and subtract the tenths:

$$90 + 1 + \frac{16}{10}$$
$$- \left( 50 + 7 + \frac{8}{10} \right)$$
$$\overline{\phantom{xxxxxxxxxxxx}}$$

Before subtracting, we can also notice that in the ones place 7 is greater than 1, so we will need to take 1 ten from the tens place and convert it to 10 ones:

$$80 + 11 + \frac{16}{10}$$
$$- \left( 50 + 7 + \frac{8}{10} \right)$$
$$\overline{\phantom{xxxxxxxxxxxx}}$$

Now, subtract:

$$80+11+\frac{16}{10}$$
$$-\left(50+7+\frac{8}{10}\right)$$
$$30+5+\frac{8}{10}$$

We now have our difference: 34.8.

Another way to keep track of place value uses place value charts. The two problems from above are shown again here:

| | Tens | Ones | Tenths |
|---|---|---|---|
| | 2 | 7 | 9 |
| + | 3 | 1 | 5 |
| | 5 | 8 | 14 |

| | Tens | Ones | Tenths |
|---|---|---|---|
| | ~~9~~ 8 | ~~2~~ 11 | 16 |
| − | 5 | 7 | 8 |
| | 3 | 4 | 8 |

Place value tables work especially well for numbers with 0's, which may confuse students in setting up the problem. For example, 2,060.7 + 104.03 is written as:

| | Thousands | Hundreds | Tens | Ones | Tenths | Hundredths |
|---|---|---|---|---|---|---|
| | 2 | 0 | 6 | 0 | 7 | |
| + | | 1 | 0 | 4 | 0 | 3 |
| | 2 | 1 | 6 | 4 | 7 | 3 |

Now let's switch over to multiplication and division, where visual models are the ideal tools.

For multiplication, let's try using an area model. To multiply 2.3 × 4.2, you can illustrate it like this:

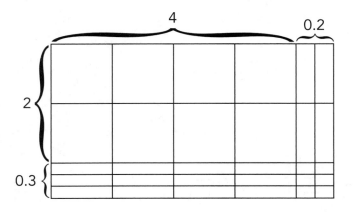

Notice that in this diagram, the lengths are *not* drawn to scale. That is, a length of 1 is not literally 10 times as long as $\frac{1}{10}$. That is all right, as long as we understand how to use the diagram.

Each of the large squares in the upper-left portion of this diagram represents 1 whole, or $1 \times 1$, because the length and width of these squares are all 1. The skinny rectangles in the lower-left and upper-right portions each represent $\frac{1}{10}$, because their dimensions are $1 \times \frac{1}{10}$. The tiny squares in the lower right corner each represent $\frac{1}{100}$, because their dimensions are $\frac{1}{10} \times \frac{1}{10}$ .

To find the product of $2.3 \times 4.2$, add up all of the smaller rectangles.

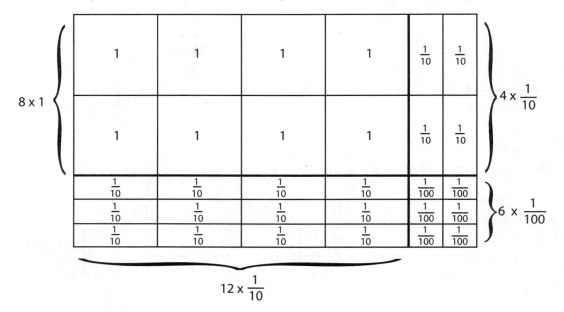

So the product is $8 + \dfrac{4}{10} + \dfrac{12}{10} + \dfrac{6}{100} = 8 + \dfrac{16}{10} + \dfrac{6}{100} = 8 + 1 + \dfrac{6}{10} + \dfrac{6}{100} = 9 + \dfrac{6}{10} + \dfrac{6}{100} = 9.66.$

You can also multiply to find the area of each smaller rectangle by place value. (This model is drawn to scale to get a sense of the actual area of $2.3 \times 4.2$, but models you use do not need to be.)

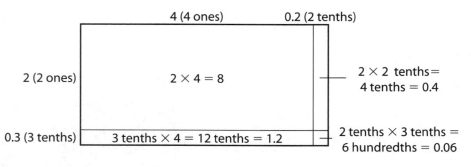

Division can be performed by reversing an area model, as shown in Lesson 2 for whole numbers. This is a valid way to divide decimals, but it may be easier to use number lines or bars to perform division.

To use a number line for a problem like 3.2 ÷ 0.8 = 4, draw the dividend on the number line. Be sure to make tenths within each whole.

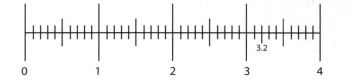

3.2 ÷ 0.8 = 4 asks the question *How many times does 8 tenths go into 3 and 2 tenths?* In order to find out, we need to mark groups of 8 tenths:

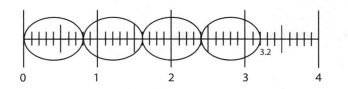

There are 4 groups of 8 tenths in 3.2, so 3.2 ÷ 0.8 = 4.

A division problem like 1.8 ÷ 3 asks *How big is each piece if 1.8 is cut into 3 equal pieces?* To find out, we need to draw 1.8 in any form, and find a way to cut it equally. This may require some amount of guess-and-check. Of course, if your child is familiar with his multiplication and division facts, then he knows that 18 ÷ 3 = 6, which is a big hint.

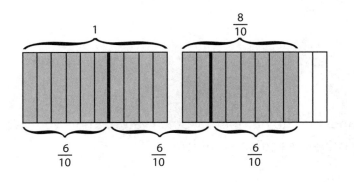

1.8 ÷ 3 = 0.6.

As always, when working with decimals, encourage your child to estimate what the answers should be before performing any operation. For example, before solving 3.2 ÷ 0.8, your child might think that since 0.8 is close to 1, the answer should be close to 3, but higher. Before multiplying 7.2 × 9.6, your child should be able to estimate that the answer will be close to 70, because 7.2 is close to 7, and 9.6 is close to 10. Performing estimates like this is a great habit to get your child into, and the sooner the better. It will help her understand how numbers and operations work, which will be critical for her later math work.

# Quiz

1. Find 15.7 + 9.72 by decomposing the number by place value. Show your work.

2. Find 9.53 − 4.6 using a place value chart. Show your work.

3. Find 5.3 × 2.4 using an area model. Show your work.

4. Find 4.8 ÷ 0.8 using a number line model. Show your work.

5. Find 3.6 ÷ 12 using a bar model. Show your work.

# 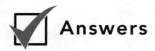 Answers

*1.* Find 15.7 + 9.72 by decomposing the number by place value. Show your work.
*The sum is 25.42. Use place value for addition problems:*

$$10 + 5 + \frac{7}{10} + 9 + \frac{7}{10} + \frac{2}{100} = 10 + 5 + 9 + \frac{7}{10} + \frac{7}{10} + \frac{2}{100} = 10 + 14 + \frac{14}{10}$$

$$+ \frac{2}{100} = 24 + 1 + \frac{4}{10} + \frac{2}{100} = 25 + \frac{4}{10} + \frac{2}{100} = 25.42$$

*If your child is familiar with the old-fashioned "carry the one" algorithm, he may make errors on a problem like this. Many students mistakenly write the addition in the following way, lining up the first digit of each number:*

15.7
+9.7
‾‾‾‾‾

*This will cause your child to add the 1 to the 9, even though the 1 is a ten, and the 9 is nine ones. The correct way to write out this algorithm is by lining up the decimals, so that all the place values are correctly added together, as shown below. If your child does not know this algorithm yet, it is not recommended that you show him until he has mastered the place value method, which will empower him to reason with place value.*

15.7
+9.7
‾‾‾‾‾

2. Find 9.53 – 4.6 using a place value chart. Show your work.

   *The difference is 4.93. Using a place value chart:*

|   | Ones | Tenths | Hundredths |
|---|------|--------|------------|
|   | $\cancel{9}$ 8 | 15 | 3 |
| − | 4 | 6 | 0 |
|   | 4 | 9 | 3 |

*If your child is familiar with the old-fashioned "borrowing" algorithm, she may make errors on a problem like this. Many students mistakenly write the subtraction in the following way, lining up the final digit of each number:*

9.83
−4.6
‾‾‾‾‾

*This will cause your child to subtract the 6 from the 3 and the 4 from the 8, even though the place values do not match. The correct way to write out this algorithm is by lining up the decimals, so that all the place values are correctly subtracted from pieces of the same size, as shown below. If your child does not know this algorithm yet, it is not recommended that you show her until she has mastered the place value method, which will empower her to reason with place value.*

3. Find 5.3 × 2.4 using an area model. Show your work.

   *The product is 12.72. Here are two possible area models:*

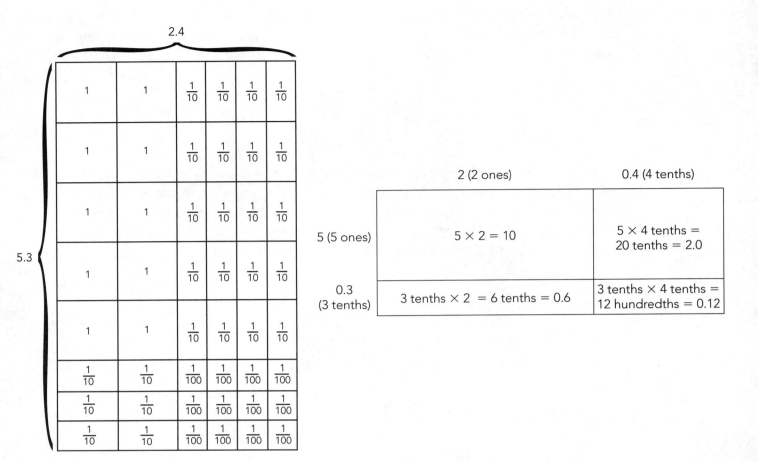

$$10 + 0.6 + 2.0 + 0.12 = 10 + 2 + 0.72 = 12.72$$

4. Find 4.8 ÷ 0.8 using a number line model. Show your work.
   *The quotient is 6, as shown on this number line:*

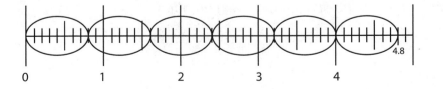

5. Find 3.6 ÷ 12 using a bar model. Show your work.
   *The quotient is 0.3, as shown on this bar model:*

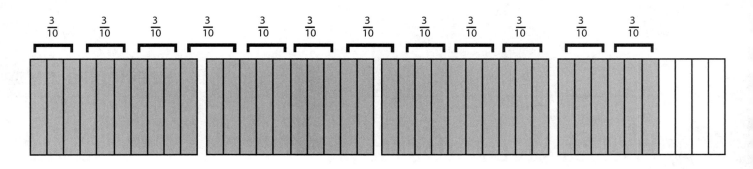

*All of these are straightforward operations problems that will give your child opportunities to practice reasoning with place value and using visual representations to understand how the numbers work together. Remember to always estimate before operating.*

*It is easy to create more questions like this for your child simply by thinking of any numbers and asking her to add, subtract, or multiply them with an appropriate model—a fun way to generate numbers is to use a spinner or dice. For division problems, start by multiplying two numbers (using a calculator if you choose) and then offer your child that result and one of the numbers you multiplied—this will make sure that the division problem works out precisely, which is expected at this grade level.*

# THE STANDARDS

***5.NBT.B.6:*** *Find whole-number quotients of whole numbers with up to four-digit dividends and two-digit divisors, using strategies based on place value, the properties of operations, and/or the relationship between multiplication and division. Illustrate and explain the calculation by using equations, rectangular arrays, and/or area models.*

***5.NBT.B.7:*** *Add, subtract, multiply, and divide decimals to hundredths, using concrete models or drawings and strategies based on place value, properties of operations, and/or the relationship between addition and subtraction; relate the strategy to a written method and explain the reasoning used.*

***5.MD.A.1:*** *Convert among different-sized standard measurement units within a given measurement system (e.g., convert 5 cm to 0.05 m), and use these conversions in solving multistep, real world problems.*

***5.MD.A.2:*** *Make a line plot to display a data set of measurements in fractions of a unit (1/2, 1/4, 1/8). Use operations on fractions for this grade to solve problems involving information presented in line plots. For example, given different measurements of liquid in identical beakers, find the amount of liquid each beaker would contain if the total amount in all the beakers were redistributed equally.*

## What does it mean?

These standards, taken together, focus on problem solving with real-life situations and multiple steps. The goal of all math classes in elementary school is to support students in using math successfully for their everyday tasks, which these problems represent.

## Try this together

One of the most important skills in this lesson is to look for words or situations that provide clues about which operation (+, –, ×, or ÷) to use. For example, words like *together* or *more* can indicate addition. Words like *less, ate, used,* or *gave away* can indicate subtraction. Both multiplication and division use situations with equal groups and the word *each*, so figure out whether you need to know the number of groups, the number in each group, or the total to choose an operation.

When working with your child on word problems, there are a few simple questions you can ask to help her see the big picture. *What do we need to find out?* is always a good place to start, because it gives focus to the process. Once your child clearly knows the goal, you can ask her *What do we already know?* Then she will know the starting point and the ending point, and she can begin to form a plan, with the guidance of a question like *What do we need to figure out before we can get our answer?*

Try this with a simple example:

A farmer counts his livestock. There are 8 pigs, 12 cows, and 31 chickens. How many feet are there altogether, including the farmer, his wife, and their three children?

First, *What do we need to find out?* We are looking for the total number of feet, including all the animals and people.

Second, *What do we already know?* We know the exact number of each type of animal, and the number of people. We also know how many feet each animal or person has, which is *not* stated in the problem.

Now we can form a plan: *What do we need to figure out before we can get our answer?* There are lots of ways to go about this. We could start by finding the total number of four-legged animals and the total number of two-legged animals, including humans. Or we could first find the total number of legs for each group of animals. We do this by multiplying the number of animals by the number of feet each animal has:

8 pigs × 4 feet on each pig = 32 feet

12 cows × 4 feet on each cow = 48 feet

31 chickens × 2 feet on each chicken = 62 feet

5 people × 2 feet on each person = 10 feet

Now that we have the number of feet for each type of animal or person, we can add them up: 32 + 48 + 62 + 10 = 152 feet

Students should also be familiar with common measurement conversions, and the shaded ones should be memorized:

| Length | |
|---|---|
| 1 foot = 12 inches | 1 meter = 1,000 millimeters |
| 1 yard = 3 feet | 1 kilometer = 1,000 meters |
| 1 mile = 1,760 yards | |

| Liquid Volume | |
|---|---|
| 1 cup = 8 fluid ounces | 1 liter = 1,000 milliliters |
| 1 pint = 2 cups | |
| 1 quart = 2 pints | |
| 1 gallon = 4 quarts | |

| Weight and Mass | |
|---|---|
| 1 pound = 16 ounces | 1 gram = 1,000 milligrams |
| 1 ton = 2,000 pounds | 1 kilogram = 1,000 grams |

## ❓ Quiz

1. The amounts of lemonade in five different pitchers are shown on the line plot below.

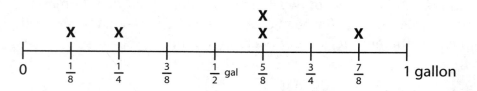

How much lemonade would be in each pitcher if all of the lemonade were poured back into a big container, and then the same amount was put into each pitcher?

2. Dylan is selling lemonade to earn money. He sells small cups of lemonade for $0.50 each, and large cups for $0.75 each. If Dylan sells 12 small cups of lemonade and 17 large cups, how much money has he earned?

3. Yosef has a gallon of lemonade in a jug. He shares the lemonade equally between himself and 3 friends and keeps his part in the jug. He later adds 1 pint to what is left in the jug. How many cups of lemonade are in the jug?

4. Amira's lemonade recipe uses 16 lemons to make one gallon of lemonade. She needs to make a lot of lemonade for her school's field day. She spends $144 buying the lemons. If lemons cost $\frac{1}{3}$ of a dollar each, how much lemonade can Amira make?

5. Natoshia is 4 feet, 8 inches tall. Karen is 55 inches tall. Rebecca is $4\frac{5}{6}$ feet tall. Who is the tallest of the three?

## ✓ Answers

*1.* The amounts of lemonade in five different pitchers are shown on the line plot below.

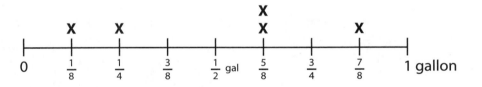

How much lemonade would be in each pitcher if all of the lemonade were poured back into a big container, and then the same amount was put into each pitcher?
*The answer is ½ gallon.*
*The clue "all" is a clue to add, and the clue "same amount" is a clue to divide:*

*The total amount is* $\frac{1}{8} + \frac{2}{8} + \frac{5}{8} + \frac{5}{8} + \frac{7}{8} = \frac{20}{8} = \frac{5}{2}$

*Now, divide by the number of pitchers:* $\frac{5}{2} \div 5 = \frac{1}{2}$ *gallon in each pitcher.*

*To solve it with a visual model, draw all five pitchers (or bar models) with the appropriate amount of lemonade:*

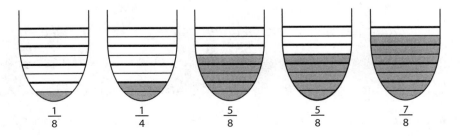

*From this diagram, we can count the total number of eighths, which is 20. If we were to share 20 eighths equally in 5 pitchers, there would be 4 eighths in each pitcher.* $\dfrac{4}{8} = \dfrac{1}{2}$

*This is an example of the kind of problem where students will be asked to analyze data from a line plot. It requires the student to use some knowledge of equivalent fractions, as well as operations with fractions: addition and division.*

2.  Dylan is selling lemonade to earn money. He sells small cups of lemonade for $0.50 each, and large cups for $0.75 each. If Dylan sells 12 small cups of lemonade and 17 large cups, how much money has he earned?

    *The answer is $18.75.*

    *The clue each describes multiplication. Find the total amount that Dylan earned from the small cups, and the total amount he earned from the large cups, and then add these two together.*

    *12 small cups × 0.50 = $6.00*
    *17 large cups × 0.75 = $12.75*
    *Total = $6.00 + $12.75 = $18.75.*

    *This multi-step problem requires your child to make a plan in several steps. Multiplication and addition of decimals is also required.*

3.  Yosef has a gallon of lemonade in a jug. He shares the lemonade equally between himself and 3 friends. He later adds 1 pint to what is left in the jug. How many cups of lemonade are in the jug?

    *The answer is 6 cups. After sharing equally between 4 people, Yosef has 1 quart left (1/4 of a gallon). 1 quart is 4 cups. The pint that he adds is another 2 cups, leaving him with a total of 6 cups.*

    *This multi-step problem requires an understanding of standard units of measure. Make sure that your child has memorized the more common ones, and understands that tests often make conversion tables available.*

4.  Amira's lemonade recipe uses 16 lemons to make one gallon of lemonade. She needs to make a lot of lemonade for her school's field day. She spends $144 buying the lemons. If lemons cost $\dfrac{1}{3}$ of a dollar each, how much lemonade can Amira make?

    *The answer is 27 gallons.*

    *We need to find out how many gallons of lemonade Amira can make. In order to do that, we first need to know how many lemons she can buy. If lemons cost $\dfrac{1}{3}$ of a dollar each, she can buy 3 lemons for every dollar. 3 × 144 = 432, so she can buy 432 lemons. If each gallon uses 16 lemons, we need to divide 432 by 16 to find out how many gallons she can* *make. 432 ÷ 16 = 27. So Amira can make 27 gallons of lemonade.*

*This multi-step problem requires your child to reason carefully with fractions, and choose the correct operations carefully. Many students will be tempted to divide $144 by 3, instead of multiplying.*

5. Natoshia is 4 feet, 8 inches tall. Karen is 55 inches tall. Rebecca is  feet tall. Who is the tallest of the three?

*Rebecca is the tallest. In order to answer this problem, we need to convert all three girls' heights to the same measure. Inches are simple to do. Natoshia is 4 feet, 8 inches. Each foot is 12 inches, so 4 feet is 4 × 12 = 48 inches. Add the 8 inches to find out Natoshia's height: 48 + 8 = 56 inches, so Natoshia is 1 inch taller than Karen. To find Rebecca's height, we can use 4 feet = 48 inches again, but we now have to convert a fraction, $\frac{5}{6}$ of a foot, to inches. We can use the number line model below to find out how many inches are in $\frac{5}{6}$ of a foot:*

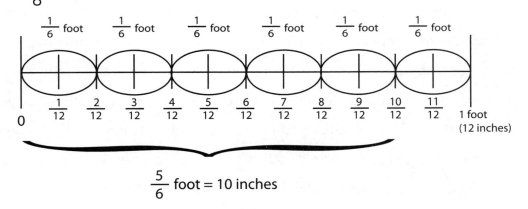

$$\frac{5}{6} \text{ foot} = 10 \text{ inches}$$

So Rebecca's height is 48 +10 = 58 inches. Rebecca is the tallest.
*This problem requires your child to compare 3 different measurements, all from the same system of measure, which are given in different, but related, units.*

# THE STANDARDS

***5.NF.A.1:*** *Add and subtract fractions with unlike denominators (including mixed numbers) by replacing given fractions with equivalent fractions in such a way as to produce an equivalent sum or difference of fractions with like denominators. For example, 2/3 + 5/4 = 8/12 + 15/12 = 23/12. (In general, a/b + c/d = (ad + bc)/bd.)*

***5.NF.A.2:*** *Solve word problems involving addition and subtraction of fractions referring to the same whole, including cases of unlike denominators, e.g., by using visual fraction models or equations to represent the problem. Use benchmark fractions and number sense of fractions to estimate mentally and assess the reasonableness of answers. For example, recognize an incorrect result 2/5 + 1/2 = 3/7, by observing that 3/7 < 1/2.*

## What does it mean?

In previous grades, your child learned how to add and subtract fractions and mixed numbers with like denominators, such as $\frac{3}{8}+\frac{7}{8}$, or $4\frac{2}{9}-3\frac{5}{9}$. These 5th grade standards introduce the process of adding and subtracting fractions that have different denominators. Since fractions with unlike denominators refer to parts of different sizes, we can only add or subtract them if we first convert them to equivalent forms with like denominators. These standards expect students to be able to perform that process with and without visual models, and to use the idea of benchmark fractions (defined below) to judge when an answer is reasonable.

## Try this together

Before your child can master addition and subtraction with fractions, she must first be proficient at recognizing and converting between equivalent forms of the same fraction—for instance $\frac{1}{2}=\frac{2}{4}$. You can practice this by using bar models. The following diagram shows how bar models can be used to show the equivalence between $\frac{6}{8}$ and $\frac{3}{4}$. Because the shaded areas in both bar models are the same size, the fractions are equivalent.

In fourth grade, children learned how to find equivalent fractions by multiplying or dividing by fractions that have the same numerator and denominator, and are therefore equal to 1. For example: $\frac{3}{4} \times \frac{2}{2} = \frac{6}{8}$.

If your child is proficient at relating equivalent fractions, then it's time to start adding. You can use bar models to add and subtract fractions when one denominator is a multiple of the other. For example, to add $\frac{2}{3} + \frac{1}{6}$, we could use the following model:

| $\frac{1}{3}$ | $\frac{1}{3}$ | $\frac{1}{3}$ |
|---|---|---|

| $\frac{1}{6}$ | $\frac{1}{6}$ | $\frac{1}{6}$ | $\frac{1}{6}$ | $\frac{1}{6}$ | $\frac{1}{6}$ |
|---|---|---|---|---|---|

$$\frac{2}{3} + \frac{1}{6} = \boxed{\frac{5}{6}}$$

Here we have shaded the first $\frac{2}{3}$ on the left. In order to represent addition, we shaded the $\frac{1}{6}$ that begins where the $\frac{2}{3}$ ends. The end of that $\frac{1}{6}$ represents the sum, $\frac{5}{6}$.

This approach works for the special case when one denominator is a multiple of the other. However, a method of converting both fractions to have the same denominator will always work. Using the model above, you can see that $\frac{2}{3} = \frac{4}{6}$, so $\frac{4}{6} + \frac{1}{6} = \frac{5}{6}$.

At a fifth grade level, your child should also be able to approach this problem by thinking about how to find equivalent fractions with like denominators:

$$\frac{2}{3} + \frac{1}{6} = ?$$  Think: $\frac{2}{3} \times \frac{2}{2} = \frac{4}{6}$

$$\frac{4}{6} + \frac{1}{6} = \frac{5}{6}$$

Subtraction problems can also be solved by finding like denominators, with or without bar models. Let's try $\frac{2}{3} - \frac{5}{12}$. Start by finding equivalent fractions with the same denominator. Because $3 \times 4 = 12$, you can convert $\frac{2}{3}$ to an equivalent fraction with 12 in the denominator.

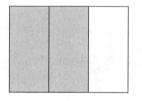

Think: $\frac{2}{3} \times \frac{4}{4} = \frac{8}{12}$

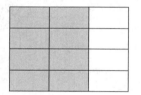

Now, subtract $\frac{5}{12}$:

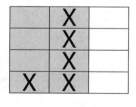

$$\frac{2}{3} - \frac{5}{12} = \frac{3}{12}$$

Here's an example with mixed numbers, $1\frac{1}{2} + 2\frac{3}{4}$

Start by converting $\frac{1}{2}$ to have a denominator of 4: $\frac{1}{2} \times \frac{2}{2} = \frac{2}{4}$. Notice that there are several different ways to show fourths of a whole, but their area is the same.

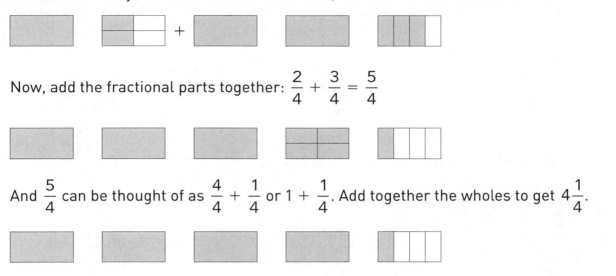

Now, add the fractional parts together: $\frac{2}{4} + \frac{3}{4} = \frac{5}{4}$

And $\frac{5}{4}$ can be thought of as $\frac{4}{4} + \frac{1}{4}$ or $1 + \frac{1}{4}$. Add together the wholes to get $4\frac{1}{4}$.

What happens when one denominator is not a multiple of the other? Both of them need to be converted to a new denominator that is a multiple of both. Let's try $1\frac{1}{4} + 1\frac{2}{3}$.

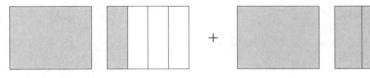

To find a common denominator, think of $3 \times 4 = 12$. Then, to find equivalent fractions with 12 in the denominator, use multiplication, $\frac{1}{4} \times \frac{3}{3} = \frac{3}{12}$ and $\frac{2}{3} \times \frac{4}{4} = \frac{8}{12}$. All of the small squares show twelfths in the bar models because each whole has 12 equal parts.

Now, add the twelfths and the wholes: $\frac{3}{12} + \frac{8}{12} = \frac{11}{12}$ and $1 + 1 = 2$. So $1\frac{1}{4} + 1\frac{2}{3} = 2\frac{11}{12}$.

If your child is comfortable with fractions up to this point, the final challenge is subtracting mixed numbers with regrouping. For example, $2\frac{1}{3} - \frac{1}{2}$.

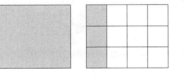 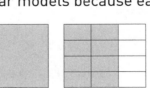

First, notice that in the denominators, $3 \times 2 = 6$, so make all of the denominators 6. Take $\frac{1}{3} \times \frac{2}{2} = \frac{2}{6}$, and $\frac{1}{2} \times \frac{3}{3} = \frac{3}{6}$. Remember that whenever a whole is divided into 6 equal parts, each one is a sixth, even if the rectangles have different shapes.

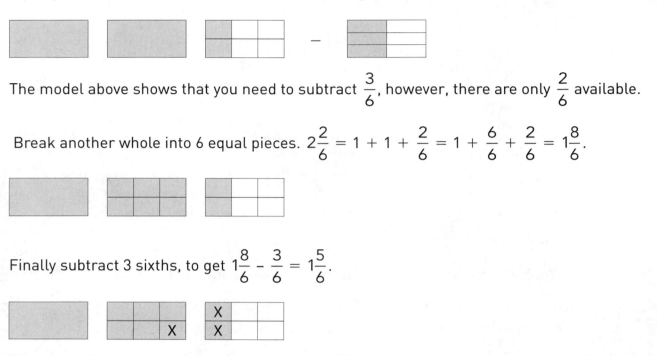

The model above shows that you need to subtract $\frac{3}{6}$, however, there are only $\frac{2}{6}$ available.

Break another whole into 6 equal pieces. $2\frac{2}{6} = 1 + 1 + \frac{2}{6} = 1 + \frac{6}{6} + \frac{2}{6} = 1\frac{8}{6}$.

Finally subtract 3 sixths, to get $1\frac{8}{6} - \frac{3}{6} = 1\frac{5}{6}$.

These standards ask students to use one more strategy, which is to use benchmark fractions to estimate. Following these guidelines, your child can estimate whether a fraction is close to 0, $\frac{1}{2}$ or 1.

- If the denominator is much greater than the numerator, the fraction is close to 0. Examples: $\frac{1}{4}, \frac{2}{10}, \frac{3}{12}$

- If the denominator is about or exactly two times the numerator, the fraction is close to $\frac{1}{2}$. Examples: $\frac{2}{5}, \frac{5}{8}, \frac{6}{12}$

- If the denominator is only a little bit greater than the numerator, the fraction is close to 1. Examples: $\frac{3}{4}, \frac{7}{8}, \frac{10}{12}$

When adding or subtracting, your child can use these guidelines to check if his answers are correct. Let's check our work from some of the problems above using estimation with benchmark fractions:

- $\frac{2}{3} + \frac{1}{6}$ adds a number close to 1 and a number close to 0, so the answer should be close to 1. Thus, $\frac{5}{6}$, which is close to 1, is about right.

- $\frac{2}{3} - \frac{5}{12}$ takes a number that's a bit less than 1 and subtracts a number that's close to 1/2, so the answer should be less than $\frac{1}{2}$. So $\frac{3}{12}$ is about right.

- In $1\frac{1}{2} + 2\frac{3}{4}$, the first fraction part is $\frac{1}{2}$ and the second one is close to 1. So the sum should be close to $1 + 2 + 1\frac{1}{2} = 4\frac{1}{2}$. The answer $4\frac{1}{4}$ is close.

- In $2\frac{1}{3} - \frac{1}{2}$, the first number is a bit greater than 2 and the second is $\frac{1}{2}$, so the answer should be a bit more than $1\frac{1}{2}$. The answer $1\frac{5}{6}$ is close.

Adding and subtracting fractions has been one of the most difficult math topics for students for generations. You can help your child by constantly asking her to use bar models or area models to represent problems, and by making sure that the illustrations accurately represent each problem.

## ? Quiz

1. Use the bar model to solve $\frac{1}{2} + \frac{7}{8}$.

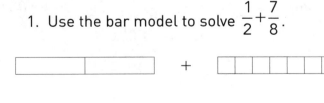

2. Use a bar model to solve $\frac{5}{8} - \frac{1}{3}$.

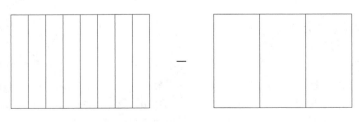

3. Use a bar model to solve $3\frac{1}{6} - \frac{1}{2}$.

4. Which of the following is the correct solution for $\frac{1}{3} + \frac{3}{5} = ?$

   A. $\frac{4}{8}$       B. $\frac{1}{2}$       C. $\frac{14}{15}$       D. $\frac{4}{15}$

5. Which of the following is closest to the sum of $\frac{1}{10}$ and $\frac{2}{3}$?

   A. A little less than $\frac{1}{2}$       B. A little more than $\frac{1}{2}$

   C. A little less than 1       D. A little more than 1

## ✔ Answers

*1. Use the bar model to solve $\frac{1}{2} + \frac{7}{8}$.*

*The answer is $1\frac{1}{8}$. To use bar models, first draw $\frac{1}{2}$ and $\frac{5}{8}$. Then, find a common denominator: $2 \times 4 = 8$, so $\frac{1}{2} \times \frac{4}{4} = \frac{4}{8}$. Then, combine the eighths.*

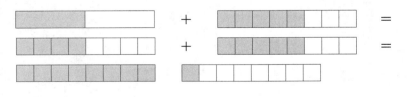

*The result is 1 whole and 1 eighth, or $1\frac{1}{8}$.*

*Questions 1 through 3 guide students through using bar models on problems that increase in complexity. Question 1 requires changing only one denominator. Question two requires changing both denominators. Question 3 requires your child to change both denominators, draw his own model, and work with mixed numbers. Being able to draw and effectively use these types of models is the key to a deep understanding of fractions.*

2. Use a bar model to solve $\frac{5}{8} - \frac{1}{3}$.

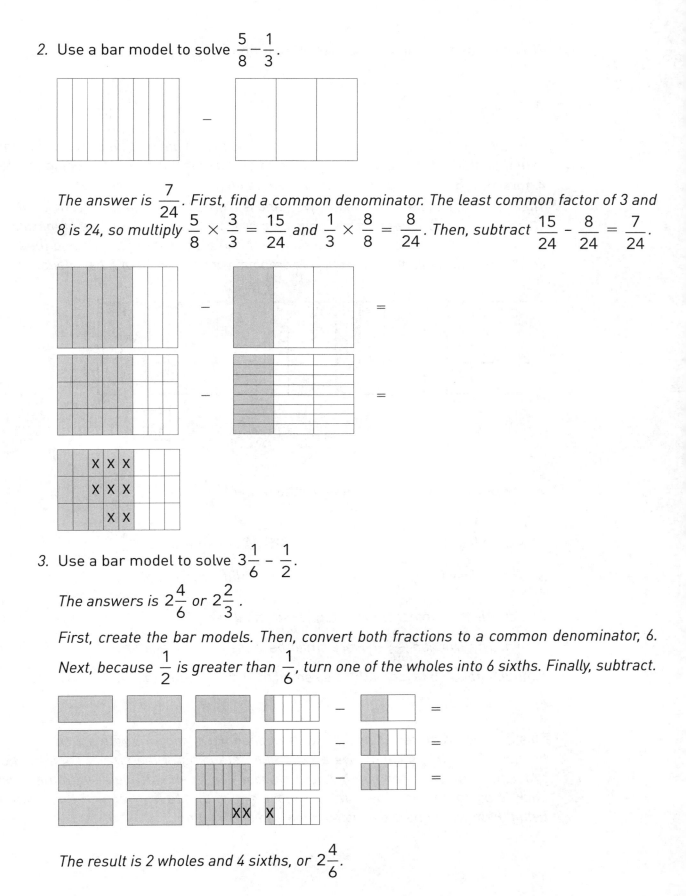

*The answer is $\frac{7}{24}$. First, find a common denominator. The least common factor of 3 and 8 is 24, so multiply $\frac{5}{8} \times \frac{3}{3} = \frac{15}{24}$ and $\frac{1}{3} \times \frac{8}{8} = \frac{8}{24}$. Then, subtract $\frac{15}{24} - \frac{8}{24} = \frac{7}{24}$.*

3. Use a bar model to solve $3\frac{1}{6} - \frac{1}{2}$.

*The answers is $2\frac{4}{6}$ or $2\frac{2}{3}$.*

*First, create the bar models. Then, convert both fractions to a common denominator, 6. Next, because $\frac{1}{2}$ is greater than $\frac{1}{6}$, turn one of the wholes into 6 sixths. Finally, subtract.*

*The result is 2 wholes and 4 sixths, or $2\frac{4}{6}$.*

4. Which of the following is the correct solution for $\frac{1}{3} + \frac{3}{5} =$?

A. $\frac{4}{8}$       B. $\frac{1}{2}$       C. $\frac{14}{15}$       D. $\frac{4}{15}$

*Choice A is the correct answer, as shown in the model below. Choice C is a common mistake that students make by adding the numerators (1 + 3 = 4) and adding the denominators (3 + 5 = 8). Choice D is equivalent to choice C, but simplified.*

*This question can be solved in any way, and is a great opportunity for your child to use the standard procedure of using multiplication by fractions with the same numerator and denominator to find equivalent fractions with the same denominators and then adding. Challenge your child to figure out this problem with and without a bar model.*

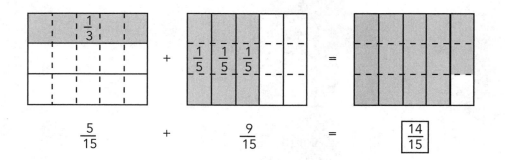

$$\frac{5}{15} \quad + \quad \frac{9}{15} \quad = \quad \boxed{\frac{14}{15}}$$

5. Which of the following is closest to the sum of $\frac{1}{10}$ and $\frac{2}{3}$?

A. A little less than $\frac{1}{2}$       B. A little more than $\frac{1}{2}$

C. A little less than 1       D. A little more than 1

*Choice C is the correct answer. Your child should know that $\frac{2}{3}$ is larger than $\frac{1}{2}$ but smaller than 1. The fraction $\frac{1}{10}$ is very small because the numerator is much smaller than the denominator. Adding something so small to $\frac{2}{3}$ will produce a sum that is closer to 1 whole, but still a little less.*

*This question requires your child to use benchmark fractions with a high level of sophistication. Your child should have a solid understanding of the size of each fraction in the problem so that she can combine them accurately. If she struggles with this problem, go back to using number lines and bar models to estimate fractions on their own and then using them to estimate during addition and subtraction.*

# THE STANDARDS

**5.NF.B.4:** *Apply and extend previous understandings of multiplication to multiply a fraction or whole number by a fraction.*

**5.NF.B.4a:** *Interpret the product (a/b) × q as a parts of a partition of q into b equal parts; equivalently, as the result of a sequence of operations a × q ÷ b. For example, use a visual fraction model to show (2/3) × 4 = 8/3, and create a story context for this equation. Do the same with (2/3) × (4/5) = 8/15. (In general, (a/b) × (c/d) = ac/bd.)*

**5.NF.B.6:** *Solve real world problems involving multiplication of fractions and mixed numbers, e.g., by using visual fraction models or equations to represent the problem.*

## What does it mean?

These standards address the process of multiplying a fraction by either a whole number or another fraction. Students should understand the connection between multiplying whole numbers and multiplying fractions, rather than thinking of them as two unrelated or different ideas. Students may use an algorithm for multiplying fractions (multiply the numerators to find the numerator of the product, and multiply the denominators to find the denominator of the product), but they will often be asked to show the multiplication in a visual form, using representations like number lines, fraction bars, and area models. They will also be asked to perform multiplication based on contextual problems, and even to make up their own story context for a given multiplication problem.

## Try this together

Mastering fractions is essential for students preparing for middle school math. The representations used in 5th grade are an essential part of that understanding. To help your child with fractions, ask him to draw a visual representation for every possible problem, until you see he understands it at a deep level. Two visual models that work well are number lines and fraction bars.

A number line is a great way to multiply a fraction by a whole number, for example, $\frac{2}{3} \times 4$. In order to represent this, we can draw a number line, starting at 0, and divide each unit on the number line into thirds. We don't know quite where to end our number line, so this is a good time to practice estimation skills. If you are multiplying 4 groups of $\dfrac{2}{3}$, then the answer will not be larger than 4, since $\dfrac{2}{3}$ is smaller than 1. So we set up our number line:

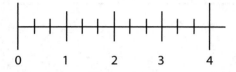

0    1    2    3    4

The tick marks between whole numbers indicate thirds. We are multiplying $\dfrac{2}{3}$ by 4, so let's mark 4 groups of $\dfrac{2}{3}$ on the number line:

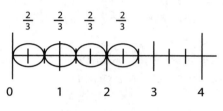

0    1    2    3    4

Notice that the 4th group of $\dfrac{2}{3}$ ends at $2\dfrac{2}{3}$. That means that $\dfrac{2}{3}\times 4=2\dfrac{2}{3}$.

Number lines are also great when multiplying two fractions together, such as $\dfrac{5}{6}\times\dfrac{3}{4}$. When multiplying fractions together, we are really asking about a fraction *of* a fraction. This problem is asking us to find out what $\dfrac{5}{6}$ of $\dfrac{3}{4}$ is. We can represent that on a number line that is divided into fourths:

0    $\dfrac{1}{4}$    $\dfrac{2}{4}$    $\dfrac{3}{4}$    1

In this model, $\dfrac{3}{4}$ are shaded. We can find $\dfrac{5}{6}$ of that shaded segment by cutting it into 6 equal pieces. It is already cut into 3 equal pieces, so all we need to do is cut each piece in half:

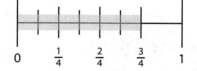

0    $\dfrac{1}{4}$    $\dfrac{2}{4}$    $\dfrac{3}{4}$    1

In order to find our new denominator, we need to know how many of these new, smaller pieces fit in the whole. Therefore, we need to cut that final fourth in half as well:

Now we can see that the whole contains 8 equal pieces, so each piece is $\frac{1}{8}$. There are now 6 pieces in $\frac{3}{4}$, so $\frac{5}{6}$ of $\frac{3}{4}$ would be 5 of those pieces, or $\frac{5}{8}$.

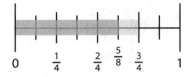

Another great way to visualize fraction multiplication is with fraction bars. To solve $\frac{1}{4} \times \frac{1}{3}$, we begin by shading $\frac{1}{3}$ of a fraction bar (which is just a long rectangle).

$\frac{1}{4} \times \frac{1}{3}$ asks us to find out what one fourth *of* $\frac{1}{3}$ is. So once we have our fraction bar cut in thirds, next we cut one of those thirds into four equal pieces and double shade one of those pieces.

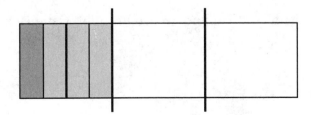

In order to find out what fraction this piece represents, we need to cut the entire whole into pieces of the same size. So each third would have 4 pieces, giving us a total of 12 pieces.

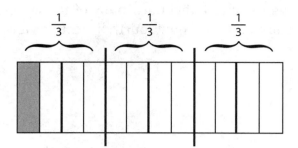

Therefore $\dfrac{1}{4} \times \dfrac{1}{3} = \dfrac{1}{12}$.

When the numerators are not 1, fraction bars require slightly more care. For example, to multiply $\dfrac{2}{5} \times \dfrac{2}{3}$, we first cut the fraction bar into thirds, and shade 2 of them. Then, we cut each third into 5 equal pieces, and double shade 2 pieces in each of the shaded thirds, but not the unshaded third, since we are only multiplying by 2/3.

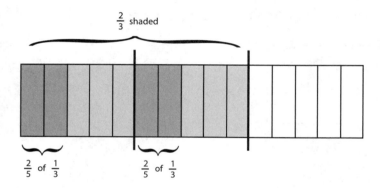

Now 4 pieces are double shaded, out of a total of 15 pieces. Therefore, $\dfrac{2}{5} \times \dfrac{2}{3} = \dfrac{4}{15}$.

An area model is another great way to multiply fractions, which many students understand better than a number line model. To solve $\dfrac{5}{6} \times \dfrac{3}{4}$ using an area model, cut a rectangle into 6 equal horizontal strips, and shade 5 of them:

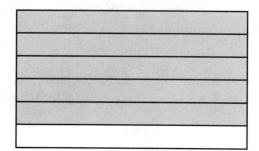

Now cut the same rectangle into 4 vertical columns:

We now have a total of 24 pieces in our rectangle. If we shade 3 of the 4 columns, we will see that some of the 24 pieces are double shaded. These pieces represent our product.

There are 15 out of 24 pieces that are double shaded. Therefore, $\frac{5}{6} \times \frac{3}{4} = \frac{15}{24}$, or $\frac{5}{8}$.

As you work with your child on multiplication with fractions, it is important to help him see that the process of multiplication is no different whether those numbers are whole numbers, mixed numbers, or fractions. For instance, suppose you are multiplying $\frac{3}{5} \times 8$. You might ask questions like, *How is this different from multiplying* 3 × 8? Remember that multiplication is equivalent to repeated addition. Does your child understand that this problem is the same as adding 8 groups of $\frac{3}{5}$ together? Does he understand that he could also think of $\frac{3}{5} \times 8$ as cutting 8 wholes into 5 equal parts, and counting 3 of those parts, as in the diagram below?

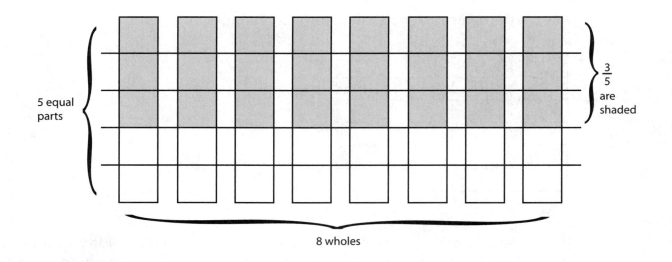

5 equal parts

$\frac{3}{5}$ are shaded

8 wholes

When your child is learning a new math concept, you can do a lot to enhance that learning by helping your child see that concept in everyday life. Have conversations with your child about where fractions and mixed numbers show up in your daily activities. Then help your child see when these situations might call for multiplication. For example, buying gas. If gas costs $4\frac{3}{4}$ dollars per gallon, how much would 9 gallons cost?

To solve this problem, let's think of $4\frac{3}{4}$ as $4 + \frac{3}{4}$. $4 \times 9 = 36$. To find out what $\frac{3}{4} \times 9$ is, we can use a number line. We break each whole on the number line into 4 equal pieces, representing fourths, and we can circle 9 groups of 3 fourths.

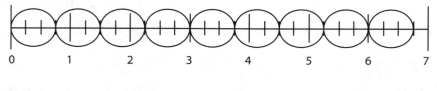

$$\frac{3}{4} \times 9 = 6\frac{3}{4}$$

Since the last group of $\frac{3}{4}$ ends at $6\frac{3}{4}$, that is the product of $\frac{3}{4} \times 9$. Therefore, the total cost of the gas would be $36 + 6\frac{3}{4} = 42\frac{3}{4}$, or $42.75.

This type of questioning will help your child contextualize this new skill of fraction multiplication in terms of his prior knowledge, and also prepare for later work on multiplication, when the numbers being multiplied are integers, square roots, or even algebraic expressions.

# ❓ Quiz

1. Use a number line to multiply $5 \times \dfrac{3}{4}$ .

2. Use a fraction bar to multiply $\dfrac{1}{3} \times \dfrac{5}{8}$ .

3. There are 10 children at a birthday party. $\dfrac{2}{5}$ of the children are boys. How many boys are at the party?

4. Mrs. Nelson needs $\dfrac{3}{8}$ of a cup of butter to make 1 dozen of her famous sugar cookies. How much butter would she need to make 3 dozen sugar cookies?

5. Multiply $1\dfrac{1}{5} \times \dfrac{2}{3}$. Make up a story to fit this problem.

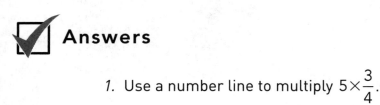

# Answers

1. Use a number line to multiply $5 \times \dfrac{3}{4}$.

   *The answer is $3\dfrac{3}{4}$.*

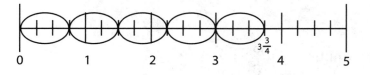

2. Use a fraction bar to multiply $\dfrac{1}{3} \times \dfrac{5}{8}$.

   *The correct answer is $\dfrac{5}{24}$. The fraction bar below shows $\dfrac{5}{8}$ of $\dfrac{1}{3}$ double-shaded.*

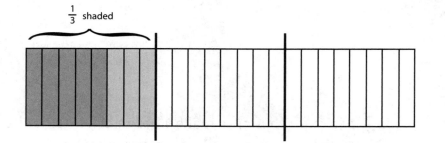

   *Questions 1 and 2 require students to solve the multiplication problems using specific vi-sual models. These models are intended to help students conceptualize the fractions they are working with in a way that will ensure they understand and master the process. The number line model in particular helps students build on their prior knowledge of whole number multiplication, applying past concepts to fractions.*

3. There are 10 children at a birthday party. $\dfrac{2}{5}$ of the children are boys. How many boys are at the party?

   *The answer is 4 boys. A number line model would work well here:*

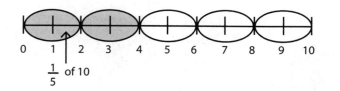

*In this diagram, we have taken a slightly different approach than before. We have divided the 10 children up into 5 equal groups (fifths), and shaded two of those groups to see how many boys are at the party. $\frac{2}{5}$ of 10 are shaded.*

4. Mrs. Nelson needs $\frac{3}{8}$ of a cup of butter to make 1 dozen of her famous sugar cookies. How much butter would she need to make 3 dozen sugar cookies?

*The answer is $1\frac{1}{8}$. A number line works well here*

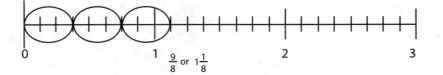

*Questions 3 and 4 provide contexts for fraction multiplication problems. Students are expected to interpret and solve real world problems like these, and use visual models to help them understand what is happening in the story. By not specifying a model to use, these problems allow your child to make the decision for himself, a process which will allow him to think about how the different models make sense to him, and which one is most appropriate for the given problem.*

5. Multiply $1\frac{1}{5} \times \frac{2}{3}$. Make up a story to fit this problem

*The product is $\frac{4}{5}$, as the number line below indicates.*

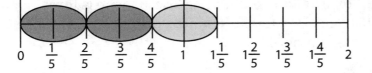

*One possible story is: A family drove for $1\frac{1}{5}$ hours on the way to the zoo. The drive home only took $\frac{2}{3}$ as long. How long did it take them to get home?*

*This question requires the student to make up a context for a given problem. This is a very important aspect of these standards, as it gives kids a way to see the relevance of the math to their everyday life.*

# THE STANDARDS

**5.NF.B.4b:** *Find the area of a rectangle with fractional side lengths by tiling it with unit squares of the appropriate unit fraction side lengths, and show that the area is the same as would be found by multiplying the side lengths. Multiply fractional side lengths to find areas of rectangles, and represent fraction products as rectangular areas.*

**5.NF.B.5b:** *Interpret multiplication as scaling by explaining why multiplying a given number by a fraction greater than 1 results in a product greater than the given number (recognizing multiplication by whole numbers greater than 1 as a familiar case); explaining why multiplying a given number by a fraction less than 1 results in a product smaller than the given number; and relating the principle of fraction equivalence $\frac{a}{b} = \frac{(n \times a)}{(n \times b)}$ to the effect of multiplying $\frac{a}{b}$ by 1.*

## What does it mean?

In this lesson we will explore two other approaches to multiplying fractions, using area and scaling.

One familiar aspect of multiplication is area. In the Common Core, students begin working with area as early as 2nd grade. Your child has learned in previous grades that the area of a rectangle is the product of its length and width. Now that she is learning to multiply fractions, this standard will require her to find the area of rectangles whose dimensions are fractions, rather than whole numbers.

Your child should also be comfortable thinking of multiplication as scaling, like zooming in or out on a photo. For example, multiplying by a scale factor of 1 creates a new object that is the same size. A scale factor of 2 doubles the size. Multiplying by a scale factor of $\frac{1}{2}$ will make the object half the original size. Your child can use scaling to estimate the result of multiplying two numbers.

## Try this together

Your child should already be familiar with multiplying whole numbers using area models from fourth grade. For review, this example shows $26 \times 49$. You can think of it as 2 tens and 6 ones multiplied by 4 tens and 9 ones.

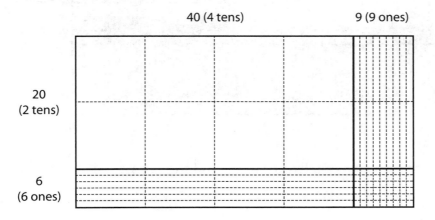

Because $10 \times 10 = 100$, 4 tens $\times$ 2 tens = 8 hundreds. In the area model, you can count that there are 8 hundreds squares, or 800. Now, multiply 6 ones $\times$ 4 tens to get 24 tens, or 240. In the area model, you can count 24 tens at the bottom. Next, 2 tens $\times$ 9 ones = 18 tens, shown on the right side, or 180. Finally, 6 ones $\times$ 9 ones = 54 ones, which are represented by the small squares. The total area is $800 + 240 + 180 + 54 = 1{,}274$.

In fifth grade, your child is learning to use area models for fractions. This area model shows $\frac{3}{4} \times \frac{1}{2}$. Notice that the large square on the outside is 1 whole and its area is 1 unit $\times$ 1 unit = 1 square unit. The small shaded rectangle has the dimensions $\frac{1}{2}$ units in width and $\frac{3}{4}$ units in height, so its area is $\frac{3}{4} \times \frac{1}{2}$.

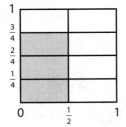

Looking at the model, you can see that it is divided into 8 equal parts and 3 of them are shaded, so $\frac{3}{4} \times \frac{1}{2} = \frac{3}{8}$.

Now, let's try it with mixed numbers. This area model shows $1\frac{2}{5} \times 3\frac{2}{3}$. Notice that each large square is 1 square unit. The height of the shaded rectangle is 1 whole and 2 more fifths. The width is 3 wholes and 2 more thirds.

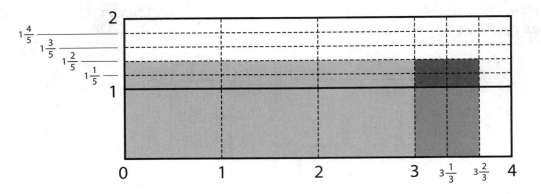

Just as we did when multiplying whole numbers, find the area of each smaller section of the rectangle. The largest section uses whole numbers: $1 \times 3 = 3$, and you can count the 3 square units. Above that are fifths. You can count 6 fifths, or multiply $\frac{2}{5} \times 3 = \frac{6}{5}$. In the lower right are thirds. There are 2 thirds because $\frac{2}{3} \times 1 = \frac{2}{3}$. And the top right square is divided into 15 equal parts and 4 of them are filled, so there are $\frac{4}{15}$. Using multiplication, $\frac{2}{5} \times \frac{2}{3} = \frac{2 \times 2}{5 \times 3} = \frac{4}{15}$.

Now, add the parts together by finding equivalent fractions with the same denominator:

$$3 + \frac{6}{5} + \frac{2}{3} + \frac{4}{15} = 3 + \frac{18}{15} + \frac{10}{15} + \frac{4}{15} = 3 + \frac{32}{15}$$

$$= 3 + \frac{15}{15} + \frac{15}{15} + \frac{2}{15} = 3 + 1 + 1 + \frac{2}{15} = 4\frac{2}{15}.$$

So $1\frac{2}{5} \times 3\frac{2}{3} = 4\frac{2}{15}$. Your child should be comfortable drawing these area models independently using graph paper with large squares (at least 1 inch $\times$ 1 inch) or by estimating with rectangles on blank paper.

The other concept in this lesson is understanding how multiplication by numbers greater than 1, equal to 1, or between 0 and 1 changes (or scales) a number. When you make a copy with a photocopier that is a different size, or zoom in and out on a picture, you are scaling. The number that you use to scale up or down is called a **scale factor**.

- Scaling by numbers greater than 1 makes an object bigger. If you start with 4 and use a scale factor of 2, the result is $4 \times 2 = 8$. The number 4 has doubled in size.

- Scaling by numbers equal to 1 does not change the object's size. If you start with 4 and use a scale factor of 1, the result is $4 \times 1 = 4$. (This is also why multiplying by fractions equal to 1, like $\frac{2}{2}$ can be used to generate equivalent fractions: $4 \times \frac{2}{2} = \frac{8}{2} = 4$.)

- Scaling by numbers between 0 and 1 makes an object smaller. If you start with 4 and use a scale factor of $\frac{1}{2}$, the result is $4 \times \frac{1}{2} = \frac{4}{2} = 2$. The number 4 has shrunk to half its starting size.

Your child should be able to look at two numbers being multiplied and decide immediately whether their product is less than both, greater than both, equal to one of them, or between them. In the examples below, notice whether the factors are less than, greater than, or equal to 1:

- Example: $\frac{1}{2} \times \frac{2}{3} =$ a number **less** than $\frac{1}{2}$ or $\frac{2}{3}$ because no matter which number you start with, you are multiplying it by a scale factor between 0 and 1 so the result will be smaller.

- Example: $\frac{7}{8} \times 1\frac{1}{2} =$ a number **between** $\frac{7}{8}$ and $1\frac{1}{2}$ because multiplying $\frac{7}{8}$ by a scale factor greater than 1 creates a larger product, but multiplying $1\frac{1}{2}$ by a scale factor between 0 and 1 creates a smaller product. So the product must be in-between.

- Example: $2\frac{1}{2} \times 1\frac{1}{10} =$ a number **greater** than $2\frac{1}{2}$ and $1\frac{1}{10}$, because if you start with the larger number, $2\frac{1}{2}$ and multiply by a scale factor greater than 1, the result will be greater.

- Example: $\frac{3}{8} \times \frac{2}{2} =$ a number **equal** to $\frac{3}{8}$ because $\frac{2}{2} = 1$, so the scale factor is 1 and does not change the size of the other factor.

Examples like this are everywhere. If you have $\frac{3}{8}$ of a pizza and you need twice as much, will there be more or less than $\frac{3}{8}$? Than 2? If you start with $\frac{3}{8}$ of a pizza and eat half of what is there, will the amount you eat be more or less? Examples could relate to food, allowance, distances, games—anything you can think of. Challenge yourself and your child to find as many examples as you can in everyday life, as well as practicing with written numbers.

**Quiz**

1. Use the area model to find the area of a rectangle with dimensions $\frac{3}{4}$ and $\frac{2}{5}$.

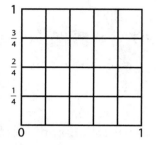

2. Use the area model below to find the area of a shelf that is $3\frac{1}{4}$ feet long and $\frac{2}{3}$ of a foot wide.

3. Which of the following is closest to $7 \times \frac{5}{4}$?

   A. 5           B. 6           C. 9           D. 13

4. Which of the following has the greatest value?

   A. $\frac{3}{5} \times \frac{3}{3}$     B. $\frac{3}{5} \times \frac{25}{26}$     C. $\frac{3}{5} \times \frac{10}{10}$     D. $\frac{3}{5} \times \frac{3}{2}$

5. Evana bought $2\frac{1}{2}$ crates of apples for a party. On the day of the party, only $\frac{7}{10}$ of the party who were expected showed up. **Estimate** about how many crates of apples are needed and then find the **exact** amount. Show your work.

# ✓ Answers

*1.* Use the area model to find the area of a rectangle with dimensions $\frac{3}{4}$ and $\frac{2}{5}$.

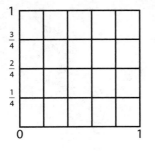

*The answer is* $\frac{6}{20}$ *or* $\frac{3}{10}$.

*To solve the problem, notice that the unit square has already been divided into fourths on one side and fifths on the other side. Shade a rectangle with a height of* $\frac{3}{4}$ *and a width of* $\frac{2}{5}$.

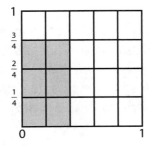

*Now, count the total number of parts in the whole (20) and the parts that are shaded (6). The product is* $\frac{3}{4} \times \frac{2}{5} = \frac{6}{20} = \frac{3}{10}$.

*2.* Use the area model below to find the area of a shelf that is $3\frac{1}{4}$ feet long and $\frac{2}{3}$ of a foot wide.

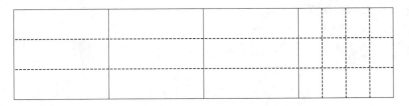

*The correct answer is* $2\frac{2}{12}$ *or* $2\frac{1}{6}$.

*This rectangle is already divided into thirds for the height and shows 3 wholes and fourths on the width, so you can move to the next step of shading. This model shows a shaded rectangle with a height of $\frac{2}{3}$ and a width of 3 wholes and 1 more fourth.*

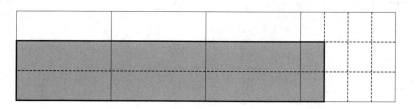

*Now, find the area of each part. On the left, each whole square is divided into thirds, and 6 of them have been shaded, so $\frac{2}{3} \times 3 = \frac{6}{3} = 2$ wholes. The final square has 12 equal parts and 2 of them are shaded, so $\frac{2}{3} \times \frac{1}{4} = \frac{2 \times 1}{3 \times 4} = \frac{2}{12}$. So the total area is $2 + \frac{2}{12} = 2\frac{2}{12}$ or $2\frac{1}{6}$.*

*Questions 1 and 2 are the kinds of questions students will be asked to assess their mastery of multiplying fractions with a visual model, with some extra support as they get started. By using area to model fraction and mixed number multiplication, students enhance their understanding of both area and multiplication. Encourage your child to draw his own models when none are provided and practice drawing them on graph paper (with 1 inch × 1 inch grid lines) or on blank paper.*

3. Which of the following is closest to $7 \times \frac{5}{4}$?

   A. 5 B. 6 C. 9 D. 13

   *The correct answer is C. Because $\frac{5}{4}$ is larger than 1, it will scale the number 7 to a larger number. Choice D, 13, is very close to 14, which is 2 × 7. Because $\frac{5}{4}$ is close to 1, the product should be closer to 7 than to 14.*

4. Which of the following has the greatest value?

   A. $\frac{3}{5} \times \frac{3}{3}$ B. $\frac{3}{5} \times \frac{25}{26}$ C. $\frac{3}{5} \times \frac{10}{10}$ D. $\frac{3}{5} \times \frac{3}{2}$

*The correct answer is D. The first factor is the same in all of the answer choices, so just pay attention to the second number, which is the scaling factor. For choice B, $\frac{25}{26}$ is smaller than 1, so multiplying it by $\frac{3}{5}$ will give a product that is less than $\frac{3}{5}$. Both $\frac{3}{3}$ and $\frac{10}{10}$ are equivalent to 1, so multiplying either of these fractions by $\frac{3}{5}$ will give a product of $\frac{3}{5}$. Only choice D has $\frac{3}{5}$ multiplied by a fraction larger than 1, which will scale it up to a bigger number.*

*Questions 3 and 4 both ask your child to use her reasoning about scaling. These questions can help reinforce that multiplying by a fraction smaller than 1 makes a number smaller, multiplying by a fraction larger than 1 makes a number larger, and multiplying by a fraction equivalent to 1 does not change the number.*

5. Evana bought $2\frac{1}{2}$ crates of apples for a party. On the day of the party, only $\frac{7}{10}$ of the party who were expected showed up. **Estimate** about how many crates of apples are needed and then find the **exact** amount. Show your work.

*A good estimate would be about 2 crates, because $\frac{7}{10}$ is between 0 and 1, so it will scale down $2\frac{1}{2}$ to a smaller amount. Because $\frac{7}{10}$ is closer to 1 than 0, it will only scale it down a little bit.*

*The exact amount is $1\frac{3}{4}$, as shown in the area model below:*

*The first two squares are divided into tenths, and there are 14 of them, so* $\dfrac{7}{10} \times 2 = \dfrac{14}{10}$.

*The last whole square is divided into twentieths and there are 7 of them, so* $7/10 \times \dfrac{1}{2} = \dfrac{7}{20}$. *The total is* $\dfrac{14}{10} + \dfrac{7}{20} = \dfrac{10}{10} + \dfrac{4}{10} + \dfrac{7}{20} = 1 + \dfrac{8}{20} + \dfrac{7}{20} = 1 + \dfrac{15}{20} = 1\dfrac{3}{4}$.

This question pulls together the skills from both standards, using scaling to make an estimate and then using methods of your child's choice (such as an area model) to show work. Remind your child that even if he gets the right answer and understands why it works, if a problem asks him to show his work, he needs to show and explain it in a way that others can understand it.

# THE STANDARDS

**5.NF.B.7:** *Apply and extend previous understandings of division to divide unit fractions by whole numbers and whole numbers by unit fractions.*

**5.NF.B.7a:** *Interpret division of a unit fraction by a non-zero whole number, and compute such quotients. For example, create a story context for (1/3) ÷ 4, and use a visual fraction model to show the quotient. Use the relationship between multiplication and division to explain that (1/3) ÷ 4 = 1/12 because (1/12) × 4 = 1/3. Note: use bar models and number line models.*

**5.NF.B.7b:** *Interpret division of a whole number by a unit fraction, and compute such quotients. For example, create a story context for 4 ÷ (1/5), and use a visual fraction model to show the quotient. Use the relationship between multiplication and division to explain that 4 ÷ (1/5) = 20 because 20 × (1/5) = 4. Note: use bar models and number line models.*

**5.NF.B.7c:** *Solve real world problems involving division of unit fractions by non-zero whole numbers and division of whole numbers by unit fractions, e.g., by using visual fraction models and equations to represent the problem. For example, how much chocolate will each person get if 3 people share 1/2 lb of chocolate equally? How many 1/3-cup servings are in 2 cups of raisins? Note: use bar models and number line models.*

## What does it mean?

In fifth grade, division with fractions is introduced for the first time. Dividing with fractions has challenged students, parents, and teachers forever. Fortunately, fraction operations are now being taught over several grades and with more intuitive visual models. There are two important concepts here: dividing whole numbers by fractions (for example, if there are 4 cups of yogurt and each person gets $\frac{1}{2}$ cup, how many people can eat yogurt?) and dividing fractions by whole numbers (for example, if there is $\frac{1}{2}$ gallon of yogurt and it is shared equally by 4 people, how much does each person get?).

In fifth grade, students will only be dividing with unit fractions. A **unit fraction** is a fraction with a numerator of 1, like $\frac{1}{2}$, $\frac{1}{3}$, $\frac{1}{4}$, etc. By keeping the numerator 1, students can focus on the effects of the denominator.

# Try this together

In division, the order of the numbers is important. In this lesson, students will divide whole numbers by unit fractions and unit fractions by whole numbers. These two procedures answer different types of questions, use different models, and have very different results.

Dividing a unit fraction by a whole number usually asks the question *If this fraction is divided into smaller equal parts, how big will each part be?* For example, $\frac{1}{3} \div 5$ asks, if you start with $\frac{1}{3}$ and divide it into 5 equal parts, how big will each of those parts be? We can answer this question using a fraction bar or a number line:

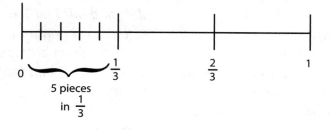

If we cut the first third into 5 pieces, then we must also cut the other two thirds to find out how many pieces in total can fit into 1 whole.

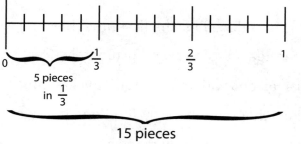

Because there are 15 pieces in 1 whole, each piece is $\frac{1}{15}$. Therefore, $\frac{1}{3} \div 5 = \frac{1}{15}$.

Your child may notice that the numbers are related by the fact that $3 \times 5 = 15$. And in fact, we are multiplying here: we started with 3 equal parts in the whole, and there are now 5 times as as many equal parts, so $\frac{1}{3} \div 5 = \frac{1}{3 \times 5} = \frac{1}{15}$.

A bar model is another great way to solve this problem. First, draw one whole divided into 3 equal pieces:

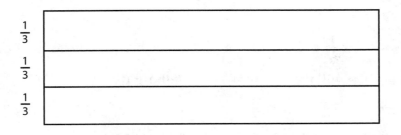

Now simply divide each third into 5 equal pieces and see how many pieces there are altogether:

Notice that dividing a fraction by a whole number results in a fraction that is **smaller** than the original fraction.

Let's look at the second procedure in this standard. Dividing a whole number by a unit fraction asks the question, if you start with a whole number and divide it into parts that are each the size of the fraction, how many parts will you have? For example, if we divide $4 \div \frac{1}{6}$, we are asking *How many sixths fit into 4 wholes?* This can be represented on a number line and a bar model:

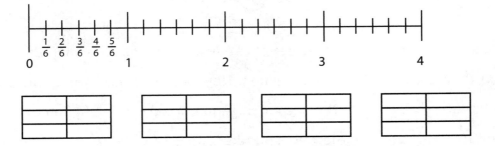

In each model, we have divided each of the 4 wholes into 6 equal pieces. Altogether, there are 24 pieces: $4 \div \dfrac{1}{6} = 24$.

Your child may notice that $4 \div \dfrac{1}{6} = 24$ and $4 \times 6 = 24$. This makes sense because you can see that there are 4 groups and each of them have 6 in them—a familiar story for multiplication. In general, the rule is $4 \div \dfrac{1}{6} = 4 \times \dfrac{6}{1} = 4 \times 6 = 24$. These rules are helpful for your child to know, but should not replace the deeper understanding that comes from using bar and number line models.

Notice that when dividing a whole number by a fraction, the result is a whole number that is much **greater** than the original whole number.

Your child will see many word problems involving division with unit fractions. For many students, the toughest part is deciding which number is the divisor and which is the dividend. In other words, which number are we dividing *by*? This is a really important distinction to make, because the answer will be very different if you do it backward: $\dfrac{1}{8} \div 3 = 24$, but $3 \div \dfrac{1}{8} = \dfrac{1}{24}$. Your child may not understand that there is a difference between 24 and $\dfrac{1}{24}$. If that's the case, ask her whether she'd prefer to have 24 dollars or $\dfrac{1}{24}$ of a dollar.

Here are two examples of the kind of word problems that require unit fraction division.

1. Tyreek has used $\dfrac{1}{4}$ of a tank of gas driving to and from work for the last 3 days. What fraction of a tank did Tyreek use each day?

2. Siani's chocolate chip recipe requires $\dfrac{1}{10}$ of a bag of chocolate chips per cookie. If Siani has 3 bags of chocolate chips, how many cookies can she make?

You should discuss the difference between these two questions with your child. The first is asking you to find a *part* of the unit fraction. Here we are dividing the unit fraction by the whole number, $\dfrac{1}{4} \div 3 = \dfrac{1}{12}$. In the second question, we are trying to find out how many times the unit fraction goes into the whole number: $3 \div \dfrac{1}{10} = 30$.

When tackling word problems, your child should always make an estimate of what the answer might be before trying to calculate anything. In problem #1 above, it should be intuitive that the answer would be a fraction smaller than $\frac{1}{4}$, since he used $\frac{1}{4}$ of a tank in 3 days. In problem #2, the answer should definitely be a fairly large whole number of cookies. If she gets a fraction for an answer to that problem, your child should realize that she's made an error.

The following illustrations show how these problems could be solved using bar models:

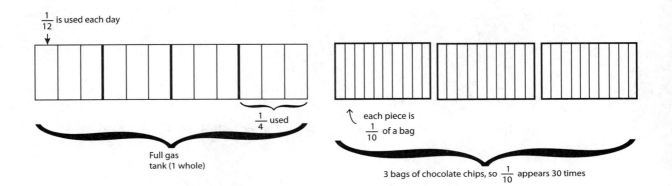

## Quiz

1. What is $\frac{1}{3} \div 6$? Show your work with a bar model and a number line.

2. What is $10 \div \frac{1}{4}$? Show your work with a bar model and a number line.

3. What is $\frac{1}{4} \div 5$? Write a story that this problem could represent and then give the answer.

4. What is $8 \div \frac{1}{4}$? Write a story that this problem could represent and then give the answer.

5. Mia has 3 friends over. They discover $\frac{1}{2}$ gallon of orange juice in the refrigerator. If Mia and her friends share it equally, how much will each person get?

## ✓ Answers

*1.* What is $\frac{1}{3} \div 6$? Show your work with a bar model and a number line.

Each piece is $\frac{1}{18}$

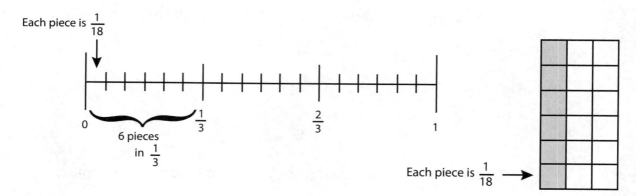

*The quotient is 1/18. This problem is asking: if $\frac{1}{3}$ is divided into 6 equal parts, what is the size of each part? These two models can be used to solve the problem:*

2. What is $10 \div \frac{1}{4}$? Show your work with a bar model and a number line.

   *The quotient is 40. This problem is asking how many fourths are in 10 wholes.*

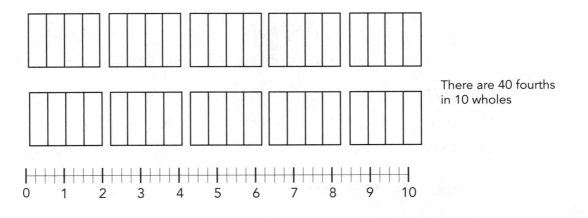

There are 40 fourths in 10 wholes

   *Questions 1 and 2 ask your child to divide a unit fraction by a whole number and a whole number by a unit fraction. Using the visual models repetitively will help your child see to make a connection between the methods, the sizes of the parts in the fractions, and stories that they could represent.*

3. What is $\frac{1}{4} \div 5$? Write a story that this problem could represent and then give the answer.
   *The quotient is $\frac{1}{20}$. The story should involve cutting $\frac{1}{4}$ into 5 pieces, or sharing $\frac{1}{4}$ of something among 5 people. For example, after everybody got a piece of birthday cake, $\frac{1}{4}$ of the cake was left over. If 5 people wanted another piece, what fraction of the original cake shows the size of the piece that each person would get? Each person would get $\frac{1}{20}$ of the original cake.*

4. What is $8 \div \frac{1}{4}$? Write a story that this problem could represent and then give the answer.
   *The quotient is 32. The story should involve looking for how many times $\frac{1}{4}$ of something can fit into 8 wholes. Money is always a great context when dealing with fourths (or quarters). Shawn brings $8 into the bakery, and each roll costs 25 cents ($\frac{1}{4}$ of a dollar). How many rolls can he buy? He can buy 32 rolls.*

   *Questions 3 and 4 ask your child to relate division with unit fractions and whole numbers to contextual situations. Being able to describe a problem with a scenario is a great way to master the operation.*

5. Mia has 3 friends over. They discover $\frac{1}{2}$ gallon of orange juice in the refrigerator. If Mia and her friends share it equally, how much will each person get?

*The answer is $\frac{1}{8}$. Start by noticing that if Mia and her 3 friends all share, there are 4 people total. Then, think about the answer: should this problem have a fraction or a whole number for its answer? Because $\frac{1}{2}$ gallon is being shared by several people, each person will get less than $\frac{1}{2}$ gallon, so the answer will be a fraction. The problem is $\frac{1}{2} \div 4$. Then use a fraction bar or a number line:*

Each share is $\frac{1}{8}$ of the whole

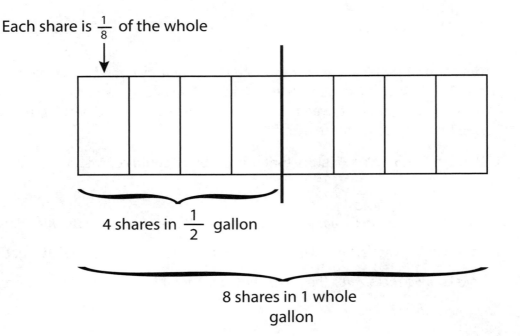

4 shares in $\frac{1}{2}$ gallon

8 shares in 1 whole
gallon

*This is a straightforward word problem. Check that your child is correctly interpreting this problem as $\frac{1}{2} \div 4$, rather than $4 \div \frac{1}{2}$. Then it is simply a matter of using a visual representation to find the quotient and making sure that the answer makes sense in the context of the problem.*

# THE STANDARDS

**5.MD.C.4:** *Measure volumes by counting unit cubes, using cubic cm, cubic in, cubic ft, and im-provised units.*

**5.MD.C.5:** *Relate volume to the operations of multiplication and addition and solve real world and mathematical problems involving volume.*

**5.MD.C.5a:** *Find the volume of a right rectangular prism with whole-number side lengths by packing it with unit cubes, and show that the volume is the same as would be found by multiply-ing the edge lengths, equivalently by multiplying the height by the area of the base. Represent threefold whole-number products as volumes, e.g., to represent the associative property of multiplication.*

**5.MD.C.5b:** *Apply the formulas $V = l \times w \times h$ and $V = b \times h$ for rectangular prisms to find vol-umes of right rectangular prisms with whole-number edge lengths in the context of solving real world and mathematical problems.*

**5.MD.C.5c:** *Recognize volume as additive. Find volumes of solid figures composed of two non-overlapping right rectangular prisms by adding the volumes of the non-overlapping parts, ap-plying this technique to solve real world problems.*

## What does it mean?

These standards will be your child's formal introduction to volume. Volume is a measure of three-dimensional space. When describing volumes, we use *cubic units*, which are units the size of a cube that is 1 unit long, 1 unit wide, and 1 unit high. A cubic inch, for example, is a cube whose dimensions all measure one inch.

In fifth grade, your child will learn to determine or estimate the volume of any rectangular prism (an object shaped like a box, rectangular on all sides) using a variety of methods. One method is to simply count the cubic units that can fit inside a rectangular prism. An-other, more sophisticated method is to count the number of cubic units that can fit at the base of a rectangular prism, forming a layer, and multiplying this number by the height of the prism. The third method is by multiplying the three dimensions of a rectangular prism together: *length × width × height*.

## Try this together

One way to help your child develop her understanding of volume is by measuring or es-timating the volumes of small boxes (tissue boxes, cereal boxes, etc.) that you can find around the house. Take any box you can find, and choose a "cubic unit," which can be any small cube you find: a die from a board game, a young child's alphabet block, or even a piece of aluminum foil pressed into a roughly cubic shape. Once you have your cubic unit, try to find out how many units would fit inside any box you can find—if you had as many cubic units as you needed, how many would it take to fill the box?

The base and height method works great when you only have a single cubic unit to work with. Suppose by moving your cubic unit around the bottom of a box, you find that 12 cubic units could fit in a 3 × 4 array at the bottom of the box:

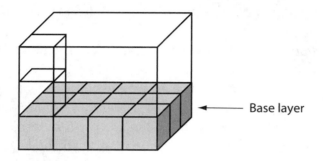

— Base layer

Since 12 cubic units fit in that bottom layer, all we need to do is multiply 12 by the number of layers that could fit in the box. Suppose the box is as tall as 3 cubic units—it is 3 units high. Then 3 layers of 12 cubic units could fit inside the box, and therefore, the volume is 3 × 12 = 36 cubic units. This method is usually less commonly used for rectangular prisms, but understanding why it works is critical for finding the volume of shapes like cylinders and non-rectangular prisms later.

Another method for finding volume is to multiply the three dimensions, *length* × *width* × *height*. This is actually the same as finding *base* × *height*, because *length* × *width* is the same as the area of the base. It is important to confirm with actual models that the relationship between the formula *Volume* = *length* × *width* × *height* is based on the idea of taking a row (the length), repeating it the number of times in the width to make a base, and then repeating that base the number of times in the height to make the whole volume.

At this point, you should continue to practice finding volumes with your child, but instead of using solid cubic units, use a ruler to measure each dimension, and multiply. If a cereal box is 8 inches long, 11 inches tall, and 2 inches wide, then its volume is 8 × 11 × 2 = 176 cubic inches. Practice this using both inches and centimeters. You can also ask your child to find the volume of a room in cubic feet by measuring the dimensions in feet. If the room is in an L-shape, it should be broken down into rectangular prisms, and then the volume of each one can be added.

Below are a few examples of some problem types this standard will require your child to solve.

**Quiz**

1. Patrick is trying to find the volume of a gift box. He finds that 20 cubes that are each 1 cubic inch can fit perfectly in the bottom of the box. The box is 7 inches tall. What is the volume of the box?

2. What is the volume of the rectangular prism below?

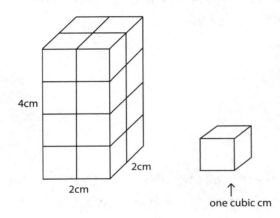

4cm

2cm

2cm

↑
one cubic cm

3. Mr. J wants to raise chickens in his backyard. What is the volume of the rectangular enclosure shown below?

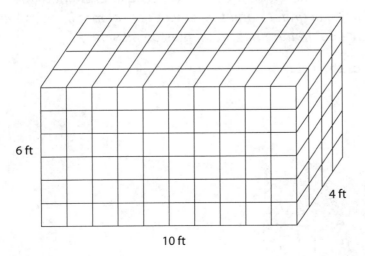

6 ft

4 ft

10 ft

4. What is the volume of the L-shaped figure below?

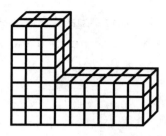

5. The volume of a box is 2,880 cubic centimeters. The base of the box has an area of 180 square centimeters. What is the height of the box?

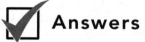 Answers

1. Patrick is trying to find the volume of a gift box. He finds that 20 cubes that are each 1 cubic inch can fit perfectly in the bottom of the box. The box is 7 inches tall. What is the volume of the box?

   *The correct answer is 140 cubic inches. You can use the formula V = b × h, where b is the number of cubes that fit in the base layer, and h is the height of the box. In this case, b = 20, and h = 7.*

   *This question asks your child to find the volume of a box by multiplying the height of the box by the number of cubes that fit on the base, which is equivalent to the area of the base. This idea will help your child understand the concept of volume in ways that will help later, when working with shapes that are not rectangles on all sides.*

2. What is the volume of the rectangular prism below?

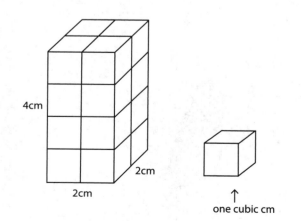

*The correct answer is 16 cubic centimeters. Use the formula $V = l \times w \times h$. The length and width are both 2 cm, and the height is 4 cm, so the volume is 2 cm $\times$ 2 cm $\times$ 4 cm = 16 cm³.*

*Question 2 asks your child to find the volume of a given rectangular prism, given a picture. In this case, any method is viable. If your child is good at visualizing 3-D objects, she may simply count the cubic units that can fit inside, particularly for a prism like this one. Otherwise, she might find the number of cubic units that fit in the base layer (or, equivalently, the top layer, which is easier to see), and multiply by the height. Finally, she may multiply the three dimensions together. This is the simplest method, but also the one that requires the most conceptual understanding in order to make sense of the multiplication.*

3. Mr. J wants to raise chickens in his backyard. What is the volume of the rectangular enclosure shown below?

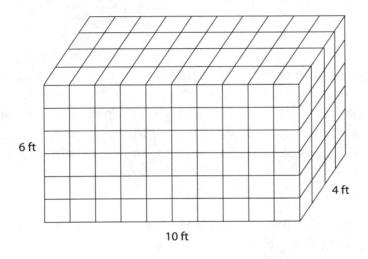

6 ft

4 ft

10 ft

*The correct answer is 240 cubic feet. Multiply the length, width, and height all together: 10 ft $\times$ 4 ft $\times$ 6 ft = 240 ft³.*

*Question 3 is similar to Question 2, but with a context added. The process is the same, however with a much larger rectangular prism it may be difficult to count all the cubic units in the entire shape, or even in the base layer. For this problem, your child should be most comfortable multiplying length $\times$ width $\times$ height.*

4. What is the volume of the L-shaped figure below?

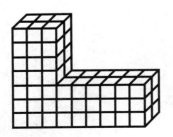

*The correct answer is 78 cubic units. This is a composite figure, made up of two rectangular prisms. It can be broken up into two rectangular prisms as follows:*

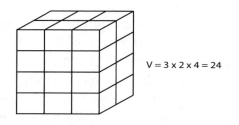

V = 3 x 2 x 4 = 24

V = 9 x 2 x 3 = 54

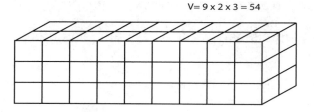

*The volume of the upper rectangular prism is 24 cubic units. The volume of the lower rectangular prism is 54 cubic units. Therefore, the volume of the original L-shape is 24 + 54 = 78 cubic units. (The shape could also be broken up in other ways.)*

*This question addresses the additive nature of volume, as referenced in Standard 5.MD.C.5c. Students need to be able to recognize that a figure with a complex shape can be broken into smaller pieces whose volumes can be found by familiar methods. The volume of the composite shape is equal to the sum of the volumes of the smaller figures.*

5. The volume of a box is 2,880 cubic centimeters. The base of the box has an area of 180 square centimeters. What is the height of the box?

   *The answer is 16 centimeters. Use the formula V = b × h. We know the area of the base (b) is 180, and the volume is 2,880. To find out how many layers of 180 cubic units can fit in a 2,880-cubic unit box, we can divide: V ÷ b = h, so 2,800 ÷ 180 = height.*

   *This question is an extension of the standards. The standards require students to be able to find volume, given length, width, and height, or base area and height. In this problem, students are asked to use division as the inverse of multiplication to figure out the height of the box, given the volume and the base area. Questions like this will help your child develop a beginning understanding of algebra concepts.*

## English Language Arts Post-Test

The following questions are intended to assess your child's reading and writing skills. As with the pre-test, there are a variety of question types at various levels of cognition. These are typical of the types of questions that your sixth grader might experience in the classroom, as homework, and in assessment situations. These items are **not** designed to replicate standardized tests used to assess a child's reading level or a school's progress in helping the child achieve grade level.

A grid at the end provides the main Common Core standard assessed, as well as a brief explanation of the correct answers. This is intended to help you consider how your child is doing in reading and writing after you have presented the lessons in this book. Keep in mind, however, that building reading and writing skills is an ongoing process. The best way to build these skills is to continue to read and write. If the post-test identifies areas in which your child needs improvement, review the strategies in the lessons and continue to focus on these areas when you read with your child.

For each section, read the passage and then answer the questions that follow.

 ## The Trail of Tears

The Trail of Tears marks an especially dark chapter in American history. "Trail of Tears" refers to the westward paths that American Indians took as part of a forced relocation during the 1830s. The Trail of Tears is just one of many similar episodes in the United States' history of poor treatment of American Indians.

In the early nineteenth century, the main Indian tribes in the southeastern United States were the Cherokee, the Chickasaw, the Choctaw, the Muscogee, and the Seminole. These were collectively known as the Five Civilized Tribes. They were considered "civilized" because many of them adopted the habits and culture of European Americans. Still, they occupied large sections of land that were considered to be their own independent nations, and had lived on these lands for centuries. This meant that the lands could not be settled by whites. As the European American population of the United States grew, more and more white settlers began to call for opening Indian lands for settlement. The Indian tribes, however, wanted to retain these lands for themselves.

The mass removal of American Indians from the southeastern United States came about mainly due to two government actions. First, the Indian Removal Act of 1830 gave President Andrew Jackson the authority to make treaties with the various tribes. The goal of these treaties was to relocate the tribes west of the Mississippi River. This would free up huge sections of land for white settlers in Georgia, Florida, Alabama, and Mississippi. Even though most members of the Five Civilized Tribes opposed relocation, government officials found some members willing to sign treaties on behalf of their entire tribe. The U.S. government ruled that these treaties were valid, even though most tribe members did not approve.

The following year, the Supreme Court ruled on a case involving the Cherokee and the state of Georgia. Georgia officials had passed laws to strip American Indians of their rights, in an attempt to force them out of the state. Representatives of the Cherokee argued that because they were part of their own separate nation, they were not bound by Georgia's laws. The Supreme Court disagreed that the Cherokee Nation was truly a "foreign nation." This cleared the way for states to pass laws discriminating against American Indians. In addition, most American Indians were not considered American citizens, which made it easier to strip away their rights.

The tribes were marched from their lands in groups throughout the 1830s. They were taken to Indian Territory, much of which is in present-day Oklahoma. Most made the thousand-mile journey on foot, often through snow. Almost fifty thousand American Indians were forced along the Trail of Tears, and at least ten thousand died during the frigid and difficult journey. Many white Americans felt at the time that the United States would never extend west beyond the Mississippi River. Because of this, they believed that they had put an end to their conflicts with American Indians. Unfortunately, as white settlements continued to expand west, the tribal lands in Indian Territory were repeatedly cut down to ever smaller sizes. The land left for Indian reservations was usually barren and impossible to farm. Nowadays, few Americans realize that well-known tribes such as the Cherokee originally came from Georgia rather than Oklahoma.

# Questions

1. Which of the following sums up the author's main opinion of the situation described in this passage?

   A. *The Indians should have adopted the traditions of European American settlers.*

   B. *The U.S. government thought they were doing the right thing in resettling the Indians.*

   C. *American Indians should have been provided with better transportation to their new land.*

   D. *The Indians of the southeastern U.S. were unfairly taken off their land and made to resettle.*

2. Based on its usage in the second paragraph, which of the following is closest in meaning to the word "occupied"?

   A. *lived on*                      B. *kept busy*

   C. *looked at*                     D. *considered*

3. According to the passage, why did the U.S. government want American Indian lands?

   _____

   _____

   _____

   _____

   _____

4. Based on its usage in the second paragraph, which of the following is closest in meaning to the word "retain"?
   A. hold on to
   B. remember
   C. give back
   D. train again

5. According to the passage, about how many American Indians were forced along the Trail of Tears?
   A. none; they went willingly
   B. about 1,000
   C. over 10,000
   D. almost 50,000

6. Based on its usage in the third paragraph, which of the following is closest in meaning to the word "authority"?
   A. credit
   B. power
   C. fame
   D. blame

7. Which of the following best sums up the main idea of the second paragraph?
   A. The Five Civilized Tribes were the Cherokee, the Chickasaw, the Choctaw, the Muscogee, and the Seminole.
   B. The Five Civilized Tribes were considered "civilized," but remained independent from European Americans.
   C. The Five Civilized Tribes wanted to expand the area of land they controlled.
   D. The Five Civilized Tribes had lived on their ancestral lands for centuries.

8. According to the passage, why were the Five Civilized Tribes known by that name?
   A. They gave that name to themselves centuries earlier.
   B. Their farming techniques were advanced beyond those of the Europeans.
   C. They adopted European habits and culture.
   D. They did not engage in warfare.

9. Based on its usage in the fifth paragraph, which of the following is closest in meaning to the word "frigid"?
   A. without emotion
   B. without fear
   C. very stiff
   D. very cold

10. What happened after the Indians were relocated to Indian Territory?

   _____

   _____

   _____

   _____

   _____

**Two Cities**

The city of Airdale sat high on a windswept peak, like a crown atop the head of a king. Its towering glass spires glinted in the light of the sun like the facets of jewels. The whole of it was bright and cool, and you could not walk three paces without catching a glimpse of yourself reflected in some surface or another. Because of this, the people of Airdale were most particular about their appearance. The styles changed frequently, aided by the fact that the city dwellers were all quite wealthy. Airdale was the administrative center of the realm, and every family that lived there was part of the engine of government and commerce. In the streets, everyone moved with a grim and aggressive purpose, unwilling to break stride even to help a lost child or a fallen elder.

Airdale was ruled by a man named Pormont, who lived in the tallest building of all. He was never seen walking the streets, but his face was all around. Crystal busts of his sharp, bony likeness watched over the busiest corners, and a gigantic statue of him towered over the town entrance to welcome—or, more likely, frighten—new arrivals. Pormont made new laws on a daily basis, forbidding people from wearing certain colors of socks or eating biscuits with their fingers or doing other random things. No one knew the purpose of these laws, but they kept the city's residents ever fearful that they might accidentally break one without knowing it.

Mossvale was a town clustered in the hollow of a valley, so low it looked like it might sink down into the trees and disappear completely. Its cottages were squat and bulbous like mushrooms, with thatched straw roofs and dried clay walls. Mossvale stayed in shadow most of the day, but hot springs bubbled into pools throughout the town and kept the whole of it rather warm. The citizens of Mossvale spent long hours soaking in the hot pools, which was the main social activity of the town. They would slather themselves with mud from the pools to draw out ill spirits, and many let the mud dry on their faces and arms as they went about their daily business. That business usually involved harvesting or cooking root vegetables, which was what the people of Mossvale ate every day. It was rare to see money change hands between townspeople. Few of them had it, and even fewer needed it. They traded goods with each other when necessary, but most were satisfied with what they already had.

Mossvale was ruled by a stout, bearded man named Rocheau who lived next to the pig stables. His hearty laugh echoed throughout the town most of each day as he stopped to chat with other residents. He wore identical brown shirts every day and only ran a comb through his hair if it was a special occasion. The only law he cared about was this: be kind to your neighbors.

## Questions

11. Based on the details in the passage, which of the following best describes Pormont?
    A. *friendly*
    B. *power-hungry*
    C. *humble*
    D. *easygoing*

12. Based on its usage in the first paragraph, which of the following is closest in meaning to the word "aggressive"?
    A. *forceful*
    B. *timid*
    C. *careful*
    D. *joyful*

13. What does the author compare the city of Airdale to?

   A. *a crown*                         B. *an icicle*

   C. *a biscuit*                        D. *a coin*

14. According to the passage, how are the residents of Airdale different from the residents of Mossvale?

   A. *They are happier and healthier.*

   B. *They are wealthier and friendlier.*

   C. *They are busier and less friendly.*

   D. *They are better dressed and happier.*

15. To what does the author compare the buildings in Mossvale?

   A. *frogs*                            B. *root vegetables*

   C. *mud pools*                        D. *mushrooms*

16. Based on its usage in the second paragraph, which of the following is closest in meaning to the word "gigantic"?

   A. *humorous*                         B. *huge*

   C. *modest*                           D. *friendly*

17. Which of the following best expresses the mood of Mossvale and its citizens?

   A. *busy and frightening*             B. *cold and barren*

   C. *rich and elegant*                 D. *warm and carefree*

18. Compare and contrast how the two rulers interact with the residents of their cities.

   _____

   _____

   _____

   _____

19. Based on its usage in the fourth paragraph, which of the following is closest in meaning to the word "identical"?

   A. *looking alike*                    B. *recognizable*

   C. *relating to teeth*                D. *hilarious*

20. Using your own words, write a brief summary of the passage. Use correct grammar, punctuation, spelling, and capitalization.

   _____

   _____

   _____

   _____

Read the paragraph and decide on the best answer to fill each blank.

(1) This morning, my mom said I could either take the bus to school _____ ride with her. (2) _____ the way to school, we passed Patricia. (3) She _____ her new bike. (4) Maryann was _____ riding with her. (5) I _____ hello, and they both waved back.

21. In sentence 1, which word is the best choice to fill the blank?
   A. and          B. or          C. nor          D. either

22. In sentence 2, which word is the best choice to fill the blank?
   A. Before       B. With        C. On           D. Through

23. In sentence 3, which word is the best choice to fill the blank?
   A. rides                        B. has been riding
   C. were riding                  D. was riding

24. In sentence 4, which word is the best choice to fill the blank?
   A. too          B. also        C. however      D. but

25. In sentence 5, which word is the best choice to fill the blank?
   A. yelled       B. yelling     C. yell         D. yells

26. Read this draft of a paragraph. Correct the grammar, punctuation, spelling, and capitalization.

Bicyclists should obay the same traffick rules as cars. Have you ever seen a biciclist speed through an intersection, just as a car is coming. I have a situation like this can caused accidents. I think bicyclists should stop when theirs a stop sign or stop light and proceed only when its safe, the way cars do. In addition, all bicyclists should use hand signals to let other's know when they're about to stop or turn. The streets in many towns and citys wuld be safer places if these simple changes were made.

_____

_____

_____

_____

_____

_____

# ✓ Answer Key

Note: The answers to open-ended, constructed response questions are sample answers. Answers will vary, but look for the main ideas to be included.

Highlight any questions that your child gets wrong. Looking at the wrong answers may help to reveal one or more standards with which your child is struggling. Even if your child has done well on this posttest, reviewing the lessons will help him or her become a better reader and writer.

| Passage | Question | Answer | Standard(s) |
|---|---|---|---|
| The Trail of Tears | 1 | D | RI.5.8 |
| | 2 | A | RI.5.4 |
| | 3 | The U.S. government wanted to make room for white settlers in the Southeast. | RI.5.2 |
| | 4 | A | RI.5.4 |
| | 5 | D | RI.5.1 |
| | 6 | B | RI.5.4 |
| | 7 | B | RI.5.2 |
| | 8 | C | RI.5.1 |
| | 9 | D | RI.5.4 |
| | 10 | Their lands were made smaller as white settlers moved west. | RI.5.1 |
| Two Cities | 11 | B | RL.5.1 |
| | 12 | A | RL.5.4 |
| | 13 | A | RL.5.4 |
| | 14 | C | RL.5.3 |
| | 15 | D | RL.5.4 |
| | 16 | B | RL.5.4 |
| | 17 | D | RL.5.1 |
| | 18 | Pormont keeps his distance from Airdale's residents, while Rocheau constantly interacts with the residents of Mossdale. | RL.5.3 |
| | 19 | A | RL.5.4 |
| | 20 | Answer will vary but should include some or most of the following points: Airdale is a city located in a high place. Its buildings are made of glass, and because the citizens can see their reflection all the time, they are very concerned with their appearance. Pormont, the ruler of Airdale, has created rules that make the residents live in fear. Their lives in general are unhappy. Mossdale, on the other hand, is located in a valley. The buildings are low and in shadow, and the residents like to bathe in the mud created by the nearby hot spring pools. Rocheau, the friendly ruler of Mossdale, has only one rule for his citizens: be kind to your neighbor. The residents live happy, contented lives. | RL.5.2, W.5.5 |
| | 21 | B | W.5.5 |
| | 22 | C | W.5.5 |
| | 23 | D | W.5.5 |

| Passage | Question | Answer | Standard(s) |
|---------|----------|--------|-------------|
| | 24 | B | W.5.5 |
| | 25 | A | W.5.5 |
| | 26 | Bicyclists should obey the same traffic rules as cars. Have you ever seen a bicyclist speed through an intersection, just as a car was coming? I have. A situation like this can cause accidents. I think bicyclists should stop when there's a stop sign or stop light and proceed only when it's safe, the way cars do. In addition, all bicyclists should use hand signals to let others know when they're about to stop or turn. The streets in many towns and cities would be safer places if these simple changes were made. | W.5.1 |

# MATHEMATICS POST-TEST

1. Alex uses $\frac{3}{4}$ of a cup of sugar to make 1 dozen brownies. How much sugar would Alex need to make 3 dozen brownies?

   A. $\frac{9}{12}$ cup          B. 4 cups          C. $9\frac{1}{4}$ cups          D. $2\frac{1}{4}$ cups

2. A school has 36 classrooms. At the beginning of the year, there are 4,572 boxes of chalk. How many boxes of chalk can each classroom have? Show your work.

3. Which is closest to $12 \times \frac{5}{8}$?

   A. 5               B. 6               C. 10               D. 12

4. Complete the area model to find $558 \div 18 = ?$

   ____            ____      ____
   (___ hundreds)      (___ tens)   (___ ones)

   | | | | |
   |---|---|---|---|
   | 10 (1 ten) | | | |
   | 8 (8 ones) | | | |

5. Kelsie is 4 feet, 9 inches tall. June is 56 inches tall. Ricardo is $4\frac{3}{4}$ feet tall. Who is the tallest of the three?

   A.  Kelsie          B.  June          C.  Ricardo          D.  It's a tie

6. Which of the following shows the correct first step in using an area model to solve 4,674 ÷ 82?

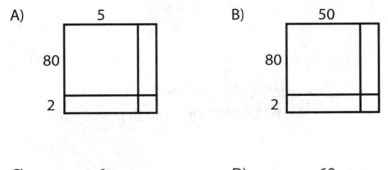

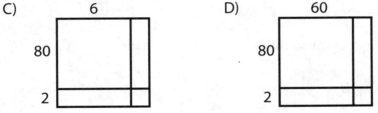

7. The graphic below represents a new home for Chad's pet hamster.

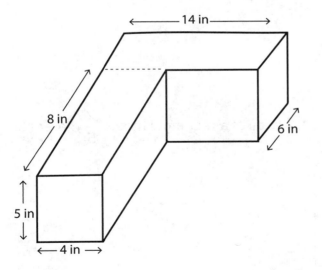

What is the volume of the hamster's new home?

8. Solve: $7.2 - 1.6 = ?$

    *A.* 6.4            *B.* 5.4            *C.* 5.6            *D.* 6.14

9. There are 20 children at the children's library. $\frac{3}{5}$ of the children are wearing coats. How many children are wearing coats?

10. Marianne buys three apples for $1.25 each and five mangos for $1.69 each. She pays for them with a $20 bill. If there is no tax, how much change should she receive?

11. Find $4.2 \times 6.7$. Use an area model to show your work.

12. What is $3 \div \frac{1}{10}$? Write a story this problem could represent.

13. Use the area model to find the area of a rectangle that is $\frac{2}{5}$ meters long and $\frac{4}{7}$ meters wide.

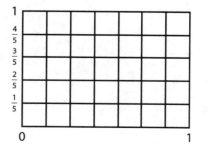

14. Which of the following is the correct solution for $\frac{1}{4} + \frac{2}{5} = ?$

    A. $\frac{3}{5}$          B. $\frac{13}{20}$          C. $\frac{3}{9}$          D. $\frac{3}{20}$

15. What is $47.2 \times 1,000$?
    A. 472          B. 4,720          C. 47,200          D. 0.472

16. Use a number line to multiply $3 \times \frac{7}{8}$.

17. Fill in the blank with $<$, $>$, or $=$. Explain why you chose the symbol you chose.
    3.2 ____ 3.02

18. Mr. Ellis is repaving the path in front of his house. The path is a rectangle $\frac{3}{4}$ yard wide and $6\frac{2}{5}$ yards long. Complete the area model to find the total area of the path.

19. The volume of a rectangular prism is 364 cubic inches. The base of the rectangular prism has an area of 28 square inches. What is the height of the box?

20. Find $3.6 \div 0.4$. Show your work on a number line.

21. Which of the following is the sum of $\frac{2}{3} + \frac{5}{8}$?

    A. $1\frac{7}{24}$　　　　B. $\frac{7}{11}$　　　　C. $\frac{7}{24}$　　　　D. $1\frac{11}{12}$

22. Which of the following will have the smallest product? Explain why.

    A. $23 \times \frac{8}{8}$　　　B. $23 \times \frac{11}{12}$　　　C. $23 \times \frac{2}{2}$　　　D. $23 \times \frac{4}{3}$

23. Which of the following is the correct solution for $1{,}820 \div 28 = ?$
    A. 60　　　　B. 65　　　　C. 67　　　　D. 77

24. At a birthday party, each child is going to eat $\frac{1}{4}$ of a pizza. If the host ordered 6 pizzas, how many children can they invite?

    A. 24　　　　B. 12　　　　C. $\frac{6}{4}$　　　　D. $\frac{1}{24}$

25. Use a visual model to solve $\frac{3}{4} - \frac{1}{2} = ?$

# ✓ Answer Key

| Question | Answer | Explanation | Standard |
|---|---|---|---|

**1**     **D**

You can use fraction bars or a number line to multiply $\frac{3}{4} \times 3$. Altogether, Alex will need $\frac{9}{4}$ which is $2\frac{1}{4}$.

5.NBT.B.4, 5.NBT.B.4a, 5.NF.B.6

|  |  |
|---|---|
| ▨▨▨□ | 1 dozen brownies |
| ▨▨▨□ | 1 dozen brownies |
| ▨▨▨□ | 1 dozen brownies |

**2**     **127**

This is simple division: $4572 \div 36 = 127$

5.NBT.B.6

**3**     **B**

Because $\frac{5}{8}$ is close to $\frac{4}{8}$, or $\frac{1}{2}$, the number closest to $12 \times \frac{5}{8}$ is approximately half of 12, which is 6.

5.NF.B.4

**4**     **31**

5.NBT.B.6

| | $\underline{\quad0\quad}$ (_0_ hundreds) | $\underline{\quad30\quad}$ (_3_ tens) | $\underline{\quad1\quad}$ (_1_ ones) |
|---|---|---|---|
| 10 (1 ten) | $10 \times 0 = 0$ | $10 \times 30 = 300$ | $10 \times 1 = 10$ |
| 8 (8 ones) | $8 \times 0 = 0$ | $8 \times 30 = 240$ | $8 \times 1 = 8$ |

**5**     **D**

Kelsie and Ricardo are both the same height: For Ricardo $\frac{3}{4}$ of a foot is $12 \times \frac{3}{4} = \frac{36}{4} = 9$ inches, so Ricardo is 4 feet, 9 inches tall, which is the same as Kelsie's height. For June, divide 56 inches by 12 inches per foot to find her height in feet: $56 \div 12 = 4$ R. 8, so June is 4 feet and 8 inches tall and she is shorter than Ricardo or Kelsie.

5.NF.A.1, 5.NF.A.2

**6**     **B**

Choices A and C are off by a place value. Choice D would have too much area, since $82 \times 60 = 4,920$.

5.NBT.B.6

**7**     **580 cubic inches**

The box can be divided along the dotted line into its original two boxes. The front box has dimensions $8 \times 5 \times 4$, which is a volume of 160 cubic inches. The rear box has dimensions $6 \times 5 \times 14$, which has a volume of 420 cubic inches. The total is $160 + 420 = 580$ cubic inches.

5.MD.C.5c

| Question | Answer | Explanation | Standard |
|---|---|---|---|

**8**   **C**   In expanded form, we are subtracting $1 + \dfrac{6}{10}$ from $7 + 2/1[$ up$]$. There are not enough tenths in 7.2, so we can convert one whole from the 7 into 10 tenths to create $6 + \dfrac{12}{10}$. $\dfrac{12}{10} - \dfrac{6}{10} = \dfrac{6}{10}$. Going back to the wholes, $6 - 1 = 5$ wholes, so the difference is $5 + \dfrac{6}{10}$ or 5.6.   **5.NBT.B.7**

**9**   **12**   Use a number line model, as pictured below.   **5.NF.B.4, 5.NF.B.6**

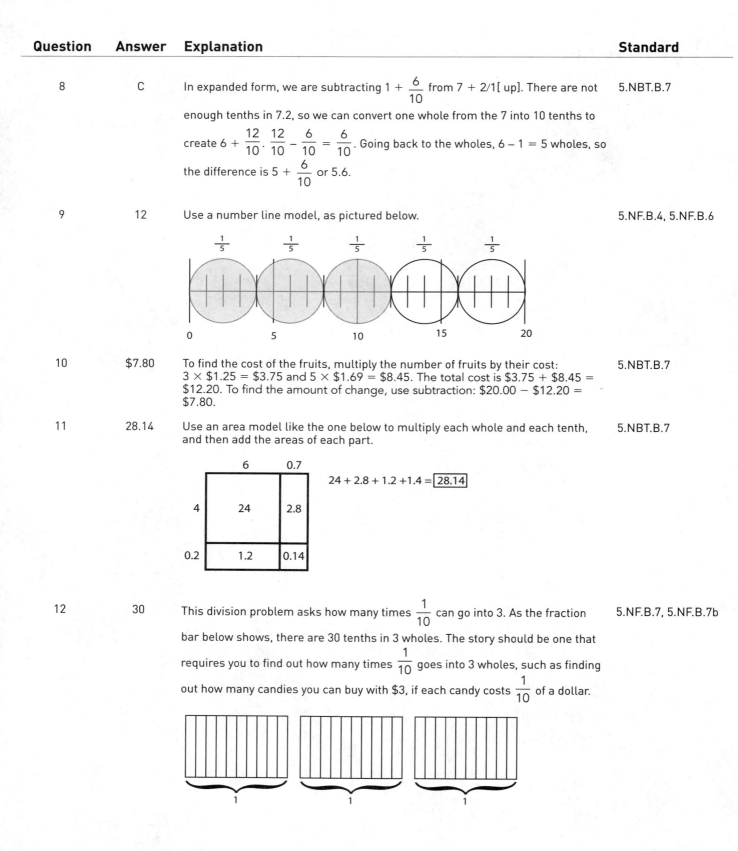

**10**   **$7.80**   To find the cost of the fruits, multiply the number of fruits by their cost: $3 \times \$1.25 = \$3.75$ and $5 \times \$1.69 = \$8.45$. The total cost is $\$3.75 + \$8.45 = \$12.20$. To find the amount of change, use subtraction: $\$20.00 - \$12.20 = \$7.80$.   **5.NBT.B.7**

**11**   **28.14**   Use an area model like the one below to multiply each whole and each tenth, and then add the areas of each part.   **5.NBT.B.7**

$24 + 2.8 + 1.2 + 1.4 = \boxed{28.14}$

**12**   **30**   This division problem asks how many times $\dfrac{1}{10}$ can go into 3. As the fraction bar below shows, there are 30 tenths in 3 wholes. The story should be one that requires you to find out how many times $\dfrac{1}{10}$ goes into 3 wholes, such as finding out how many candies you can buy with $3, if each candy costs $\dfrac{1}{10}$ of a dollar.   **5.NF.B.7, 5.NF.B.7b**

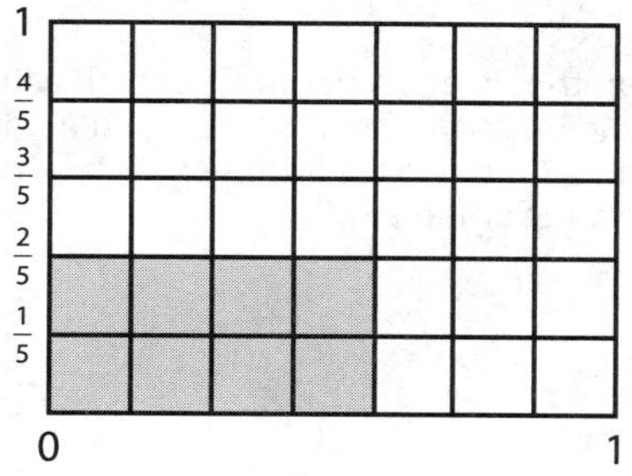

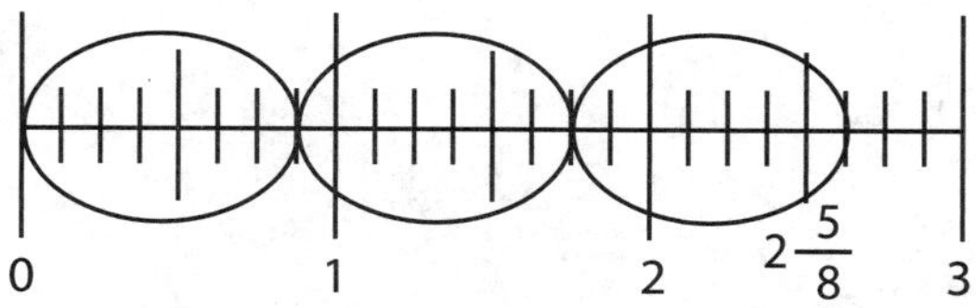

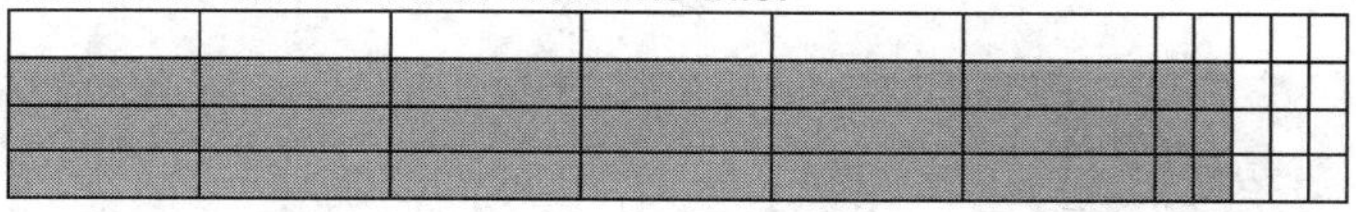

| Question | Answer | Explanation | Standard |
|---|---|---|---|
| 13 | $\frac{8}{35}$ square meters | The area model should look like this. The height is 2 fifths of a whole meter, and the width is 4 sevenths of a whole meter. In total, there are 35 small rectangle, so each one is 1 thirty-fifth of the whole. There are 8 shaded rectangles, so the fraction that is shaded is $\frac{8}{35}$ and the area is $\frac{8}{35}$ square meters. | 5.NBT.B.4, 5.NBT.B.4a, 5.NBT.B.4b |
| 14 | B | To add or subtract fractions, you need a common denominator. In this case, it will be 20, since 4 and 5 can both go into 20. When converting to an equivalent fraction, multiply the numerator and denominator by the same factor: 1/4 = 5/20, and 2/5 = 8/20. So the sum is 5/20 + 8/20 = 13/20. | 5.NF.A.1 |
| 15 | C | When multiplying by 1,000, the place value of each digit increases by 3 places. Once you have moved the decimal point right one time, you need to attach extra 0s to the tens and ones place to increase the place values of the other digits. | 5.NBT.B.7 |
| 16 | $2\frac{5}{8}$ | A number line is shown below. | 5.NF.B.4 |
| 17 | > | The first number is 3 and 2 tenths, and the second number is 3 and 2 hundredths. | 5.NBT.A.3b |
| 18 | $4\frac{16}{20}$ or $4\frac{4}{5}$ square yards | The area model should look like this: | 5.NBT.B.4, 5.NBT.B.4a, 5.NF.B.6, 5.NF.B.4b |
| 19 | 13 inches | $364 \div 28 = 13$. | 5.MD.C.5b |
| 20 | 9 | Use a number line model like the one below to show 3.6 and then divide it into equal parts that are each 0.4. | 5.NBT.B.7 |

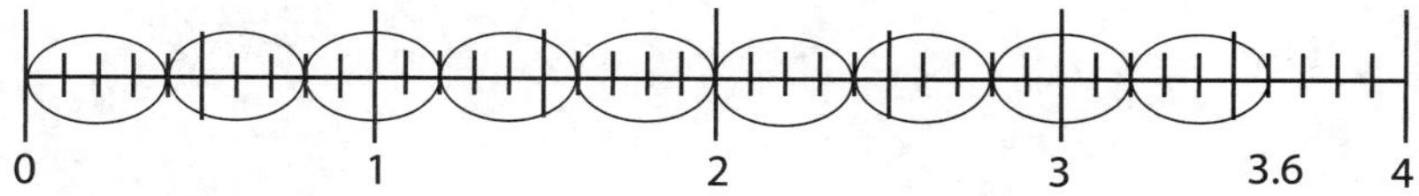

| Question | Answer | Explanation | Standard |
|---|---|---|---|

**21**  **A**

First convert to a common denominator:

$$\frac{2}{3}=\frac{16}{24} \text{ and } \frac{5}{8}=\frac{15}{24}$$

Then add:

$$\frac{16}{24}+\frac{15}{24}=\frac{31}{24}=1\frac{7}{24}$$

5.NF.A.1

**22**  **B**

Choices A and C multiply 23 by a fraction that is equivalent to 1, which will result in a product equivalent to 23. Choice D multiplies 23 by a fraction larger than 1, so the product will be larger than 23. Choice B multiplies 23 by a fraction smaller than 1, so the product will be smaller than 23.

5.NF.B.4, 5.NF.B.5b

**23**  **B**

```
28 | 1820
    -1680  | 60
     ____
      140
    - 140  | 5
     ____
        0
```

5.NBT.B.6

**24**  **A**

If each child eats $\frac{1}{4}$ of a pizza, then 4 children can share 1 whole pizza. That means $4 \times 6 = 24$ children can share 6 pizzas. Even if you don't know how to approach this problem, you should be able to eliminate two of the answer choices, C and D, because the question asks for a number of children, which cannot be a fraction.

5.NF.B.7, 5.NF.B.7c

**25**  **¼**

An area model is shown below.

5.NF.A.1